HOW TO BE AN ADULT

Psychological and spiritual adulthood does not come automatically with age. It requires ongoing and ardent work on ourselves. It involves articulating our own truth and acting in accord with its challenges.

This book can help you

—understand the origin of a reaction that disturbs you

Ask where it comes from:
- if from your shadow side, learn the art of befriending, *pages 94-97*
- if from your ego, learn to let go of control, *pages 1-6*
- if from your childhood, learn to grieve and move on, *pages 16-21*

—deal with fear

- admit you feel fear, *pages 22-29*
- feel it fully, *pages 33-35*
- act as if you were fearless, *pages 68-70*

—deal with issues in relationships

- face issues, work on them together and make agreements to improve human ties, *pages 70-74*

—understand spiritual shifts in yourself

- acknowledge gifts resulting from the steps you have taken, *pages 6-8, 89-92, 105-113*

HOW TO BE AN ADULT

A Handbook on
Psychological
and Spiritual Integration

DAVID RICHO, PH.D.

PAULIST PRESS

NEW YORK/MAHWAH

This book was previously published privately as *Letting the Light Through*.

Copyright © 1991 by David Richo

The Publisher gratefully acknowledges use of the following: Excerpt from THE POEMS OF EMILY DICKINSON, Thomas H. Johnson, ed., Cambridge, Mass.: The Belknap Press of Harvard University Press, Copyright 1951, © 1955, 1979, 1983 by the President and Fellows of Harvard College. Reprinted by permission of the publishers and the Trustees of Amherst College.

Library of Congress Cataloging-in-Publication Data

Richo, David, 1940–
    How to be an adult : a handbook on psychological and spiritual integration / by David Richo.
        p.   cm.
    Includes bibliographical references.
    ISBN 0-8091-3223-0 (pbk.)
    1. Emotional maturity.   2. Spiritual life.   3. Adulthood—Psychological aspects.   I. Title.
    BF710.R53   1991
    158—dc20   91-4496
                                                                        CIP

Interior artwork by Hiroshige (1797–1858)
Cover and interior graphic design by Frank Sabatté

Published by Paulist Press
997 Macarthur Boulevard
Mahwah, New Jersey 07430

Printed and bound in the
United States of America

To the Three Graces of my Childhood:

Grandma Angela Maria

Aunt Laura

Aunt Margaret

CONTENTS

FOREWORD

We have ever more perfect eyes in a world in which there is always more to see.

—Teilhard de Chardin

This is a handbook on how to become an adult. You may notice two themes in this book: actualizing a strong adult ego and going beyond it to release the spiritual powers of the Self. This is the "Ego/Self Axis" of Jungian individuation (see Chapter 12). It is the heroic journey *from* ineffective habits *through* adult responsibility *to* spiritual consciousness. Full adulthood includes both psychological health and spirituality.

Psychological health lies in the ability to handle one's life and relationships in responsible, joyous, and self-actualizing ways. Spirituality means life-affirming responsiveness to the here-and-now without ego attachments (though organized religion may have presented it to us as disembodied or solely transcendent).

In my years as a clinical psychologist, I have come to the conclusion that emotional and spiritual health is based on unconditional love, and that happy, mature people have somehow picked up the knack of being generous with their sympathies while still taking care of themselves. *How To Be an Adult* is a brief notebook of observations on that process—from my professional work and from my personal life—which I confide to you.

This book is written in a highly condensed way. I recommend reading it a little at a time, using single sentences or quotations meditatively. Not to rush through but simply to be with these ideas may prove helpful as you explore the angles and corners of your personal story.

Couples may enjoy reading some sections aloud and then discussing reactions.

Clients may find this book a checklist of areas to work on in their therapy.

There are ghosts asleep inside every one of us: arcane issues never addressed, ancient griefs never laid to rest, suspicions, self-doubts, banished longings, secret meanings. Something in this book may call one of these ghosts by name. It will then arise from its slumber and begin speaking. This will take the form of a sudden insight, a connection never before acknowledged, a feeling that ignites an inner chain reaction, a joyful click as things finally fall into place. You are hearing the vote of a part of yourself long ago disenfranchised. When this happens, put the book aside and listen in rapture to the irrepressible "Yea."

This music crept by me upon the waters.
                                        —*The Tempest*

INTRODUCTION:
THE HEROIC JOURNEY
OF HUMAN TRANSFORMATION

When you are no longer compelled by desire or fear . . . when you have seen the radiance of eternity in all the forms of time . . . when you follow your bliss . . . doors will open where you would not have thought there were doors . . . and the world will step in and help.

Saint Simeon the Younger said, "I saw Him in my house. Among all those everyday things He appeared unexpectedly and became utterly united and merged with me, and leaped over to me without anything in between, as fire to iron, as the light to glass. And He made me like fire and like light. And I became that which I saw before and beheld from afar. I do not know how to relate this miracle to you. I am man by nature, and God by grace." The two—the hero and his ultimate god, the seeker and the found—are thus understood as the outside and inside of a single, self-mirrored mystery, which is identical with the mystery of the manifest world. The great deed of the supreme hero is to come to the knowledge of this unity in multiplicity and then to make it known.
—Joseph Campbell

The Ego and Psychological Work

The center of our conscious life is called ego. It has two concurrent characteristics:

It is *functional* in that it is the strong grounded activating principle by which we make intellectual assessments and judgments, show feelings appropriately, and relate skillfully to other people.

1

It can also be *neurotic* when it becomes attached, addicted, dualistic, and judgmental. It then panics, controls, expects, dramatizes feelings, and believes itself entitled to special treatment. Such deception gives the neurotic ego power to keep us stuck. Psychological health means living more and more from a functional ego stance while freeing and transforming the energies of the neurotic ego through psychological work.

There are many forms of psychological work: assertiveness, processing experiences, mourning, bodywork, behavioral repertories of change, building self-esteem, catharsis of feelings, dreamwork, restructuring one's daily life, etc. This work leads to insight and to change when we are ready for it. We can trust that we will see only what we are truly ready to face. A loving balance between psyche and circumstances lets us know our work only when we have the power to do it!

The Self and Spiritual Work

The center of our entire psyche (both conscious and unconscious) is the Self. It is our inner archetypal wholeness that creates a constant balance between the opposing forces of ego. For instance, it is the Self that finally reconciles effort and effortlessness, injury and forgiveness, control and surrender, conflict with others and acceptance of them, awareness of defects and unconditional love. The Self does this because it is pure unconditionality, which is all-inclusive love.

Spiritual work means incarnating and displaying in our personality and in our behavior the unconditional love that lives so indestructibly in us and is charged with such zeal to become visible.

The Self is always and already whole and perfect. By psychological work we are *changed*. In spiritual work we are *revealed*: we manifest our inner wholeness in conscious daily life. As Carl Jung says, "It is a healing discovery to know that we are everywhere surrounded by rationally impenetrable mysteries . . . psychic facts that logic can overlook but cannot eliminate."

Spiritual work involves a set of practices that are not means to an end (as in the ego's work) but are time-honored conditions that make us apt for transformation, with no guarantee of that result. The practices are subtle: meditation, body disciplines, imaging, poetry, archetypal dreamwork, ritual, attention to inner wisdom, to myth, to meaningful coincidence, or to telepathy.

The stories of heroes and heroines tell of a journey that takes them from home, across dangerous thresholds, into new, unexplored territories, and then back home with an expanded consciousness. The three phases of this journey—departure, struggle, return—are a metaphor for what happens in us as we evolve from neurotic ego through healthy ego to the spiritual Self. The neurotic ego insists on staying in control and fears the emergence of the Self which says yes to "what is." The ego's fear of the Self is conditionality fearing unconditionality. Ironically, this is fear of fearlessness! How the ego can sabotage our integration again and again!

We let go of an attachment to illusions; this is departure. We work on ourselves to become clear and responsible, both personally and in relationships; this is struggle. We are enlightened with a higher consciousness of our real identity as unconditional love; this is return to our original wholeness.

Departure releases us from fear; struggle results in integration; return effects a transformation.

In this book we explore departure and struggle by working through the drama of childhood, by assertiveness (asking for what we want, being clear and taking responsibility for our own feelings), by dealing with fear, anger and guilt, by building self-esteem, by maintaining personal boundaries, by achieving true intimacy, by integrating ourselves flexibly, and by befriending our Shadow.

All these processes give us the power to take leave of enclosure in the constricting walls of a scared, clinging ego and cross the threshold into effective, adult living. We then move with a powerful ego (able to handle fear and desire) to a transcendence of ego that makes us unconditionally loving. Our journey is thus from fear, through power, to love!

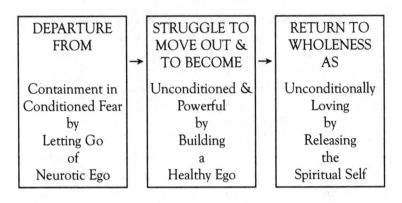

DEPARTURE FROM	STRUGGLE TO MOVE OUT & TO BECOME	RETURN TO WHOLENESS AS
Containment in Conditioned Fear by Letting Go of Neurotic Ego	Unconditioned & Powerful by Building a Healthy Ego	Unconditionally Loving by Releasing the Spiritual Self

Departure and Struggle

We are caught in ego when we are conditioned by compulsions to grasp and hold onto what we falsely imagine will make us happy or keep us happy. We then feel compelled to stay in control of the territory we fought so hard to gain.

To break free from such a tangle involves first of all letting go of the following illusions:

1. I am a solid identity separate from everything else around me. This duality is visible only to ego. As I progress in consciousness, I enjoy another perspective (that of my spiritual Self) which sees only unity and the marriage of apparent opposites.

The duality in ego vision makes me confound seamless reality into either . . . ors, good and bad, I and they. This is the source of adversarial conflict and demands that others change to fit my templates of perfection.

2. Flowing from this dualism is the second illusion: there is something out there that can fulfill my longing and answer my needs, and this something can last forever. The dualism of subject/object has thus led to the Faustian error that some person, place,

thing, belief, etc. can immure us to the changes and phases that challenge any adult. It imagines bliss to be a commodity that can be gained, lost, found, won, or possessed.

As we take the terrifying risk of letting go of this illusion we recognize that bliss is already and always in us, here and now not there and then. The only mystery is that we go on missing it.

Once we engage with the real people and real circumstances of our own lives, we discover our own inner excitement and "every day the real caress replaces the ghostly lover," as Anaïs Nin wrote in her diary.

3. Our next task is to let go the illusion that we are in control or need to be in control in order to survive. We fear the *changes* that might happen within and around us. We fear the risk that we might experience or face overwhelming *feelings*. We fear losing approval and so not surviving—a childhood equation. In fact, all fear is fear of adulthood, fear of confronting realities that we did not design or choose, fear of letting the chips fall where they may. In reality, fear is the display on our emotional screen when we type in "I am or I may be losing control."

We do not let go of control on our own. Usually, something has to happen that shows us incontrovertibly that we are not in control. From this condition of bankrupt ego, we finally let go. Great losses are thus necessary losses like the discarded sandbags that lighten a balloon so it can ascend higher.

4. The final illusion to be let go of is entitlement, the anachronistic belief that as adults we still deserve to be taken care of as we were in infancy. We may falsely believe that everyone is supposed to trust us and treat us with love and respect. We become enraged when we realize that people are not taking our wishes seriously, not acting toward us as if we were special, not loving us unconditionally. We may be applying this to everyone from our intimate partner to the driver who cut us off on the highway.

To let go of this belief is to allow the universe to deal us a good or bad hand, without complaint. "A man that fortune's buffets and rewards/Hast taken with equal thanks" (*Hamlet*). This is the humility that acknowledges every human eventuality as somehow legitimate. Our entitlement becomes humility in the face of the conditions of existence. We even trust that circumstances and crises help us advance on our path as long as we integrate them instead of interruping them. Some examples of the alternatives appear on the following chart.

I accept:	and I integrate it by:	or I interrupt it by:
Loss	Grieving	Denying, blaming, regretting
Rejection	Grieving and taking it as information	Losing self-esteem or avenging myself on another
My Mistakes	Amending	Shifting responsibility or covering up or having remorse without amends
Illness	Seeking healing techniques	Denying or despairing
Natural Disaster	Rebuilding	Playing the victim role

Effort and Grace

In the hero stories, the call to go on a journey takes the form of a loss, a depression, an error, a wound, an unexplainable longing, or a sense of a mission. When any of these happens to us, we are being summoned to make a transition. It will always mean leaving something behind, but as Meister Eckhart says, "everything is meant to be lost, that the soul may stand in unhampered nothing-ness." The paradox here is that loss is a path to gain.

To cooperate with the call is to let go of illusions and integrate whatever happens by personal work. What a plight for us humans: our task is to let go and take hold at the same time! But every hero who makes this ambiguous effort also receives the aid of a god, a metaphor for grace, a guidance not of our own making, a power that cannot be willed. Consciousness elicits graces to match every accepted challenge with newfound adequate strength. (These graces are the psychic equivalent of "quantum leaps" in physical evolution.) Our effortful steps are thus advanced by an effortless shift. This felicitous combination precisely defines the truly heroic, i.e. to put out the effort to live through pain and to be spontane-ously transformed by it. Then we are not "dragged along by fate to that inescapable goal we might have reached walking upright," as Jung reminds us.

Return with the Light

To return is to achieve our destiny: the articulation in con-scious life of the unconscious powers within us. The neurotic ego has been functional and now serves the spiritual Self. This Self is not unique and discrete. It is the same in everyone. The gift we bring home is our own awakening to oneness with humanity and nature. "In the ever-present light of no-boundary awareness, what we once imagined to be the isolated self in here turns out to be all of a piece with the cosmos out there," says Ken Wilber.

This realization makes the love we show universal and uncon-ditional. Now we understand that love is our true identity beyond ego. Like all heroic journeys our work has ended where we began! Hakuin, the Zen poet, perfectly sums it up: "All beings are from the very beginning enlightened: This very body the Buddha, this very place the lotus paradise."

Like Ulysses, we left the familiar comforts of Ithaca thinking our journey was to Troy, only to find that the struggle there was simply a ploy to bring us back home as seasoned, wise, and truly regal.

Like the prodigal son, we left the familiar routine of our father's house thinking our journey was to a far-off country, only to find that it was a path to bring us back home but this time able to give and receive a luminous, unconditional love.

> Miracles . . . rest not so much upon . . . healing power coming suddenly near us from afar but upon our perceptions being made finer, so that, for a moment, our eyes can see . . . what is there around us always.
>
> —Willa Cather

Each chapter in this book addresses and integrates all three phases of the heroic journey. Nevertheless, the chapters are arranged in accord with their main focus on each of the three themes. The following may be helpful in mapping your journey:

Parts One and Two (Chapters 1 through 8) cover the first theme:

DEPARTURE from and STRUGGLE through the Neurotic Ego to the Functional Ego.

- The PERSONAL DIMENSION OF PSYCHOLOGICAL WORK:
  Chapters 1 through 6.
- The RELATIONSHIP DIMENSION OF PSYCHOLOGICAL WORK:
  Chapters 7 and 8.

Part Three (Chapters 9 through 13) explores the third theme:

RETURN TO WHOLENESS WITH EXPANDED SPIRITUAL CONSCIOUSNESS.

part one
Personal Work

1. GROWING PAINS & GROWING UP

The home we leave, the home we build, the home we heal:
How our childhood experiences affect our adult
relationships.

Basic Needs

We are born with inalienable emotional needs for love, safety, acceptance, freedom, attention, validation of our feelings, and physical holding. Healthy identity is based on the fulfillment of these needs. "Only if someone has her arms around the infant . . . can the 'I am' moment be endured or rather risked," says D.W. Winnicott. The origin of our identity is love.

These needs are felt and remembered cellularly throughout our lives, though we may not always be intellectually aware of them. They were originally experienced in a survival context of dependency. We may still feel, as adults, that our very survival is based on finding someone to fulfill our basic needs.

But early, primal needs can be fulfilled fully only in childhood (since only then were we fully dependent). In adulthood the needs can be fulfilled only flexibly or partially, since we are interdependent and our needs are no longer connected to survival.

The Adult Whose Needs Were Mostly Met in Childhood . . .

- Is satisfied with reasonable dividends of need-fulfillment in relationships.
- Knows how to love unconditionally and yet tolerates no abuse or stuckness in relationships.

- Changes the locus of trust from others to himself so that he receives loyalty when others show it and handles disappointment when others betray.

The Adult Whose Needs Were Mostly Not Met in Childhood . . .

- Exaggerates the needs so that they become insatiable or addictive.
- Creates situations that reenact the original hurts and rejections, seeks relationships that stimulate and maintain self-defeating beliefs rather than relationships that confront and dispel them.
- Refuses to notice how abused or unhappy she is and uses the pretext of hoping for change or of coping with what is unchanging.
- Lets her feelings go underground. "If the only safe thing for me was to let my feelings disappear, how can I now permit the self-exposure and vulnerability it takes to be loved?"
- Repeats the childhood error of equating negative attention with love or neurotic anxiousness with solicitude.
- Is afraid to receive the true love, self-disclosure, or generosity of others. In effect: cannot receive now what was not received originally.

The Child Within

Our problem is not that as children our needs were unmet, but that as adults they are still unmourned! The hurt, bereft, betrayed Child is still inside of us, wanting to cry for what he missed and wanting thereby to let go of the pain and the stressful present neediness he feels in relationships. In fact, neediness itself tells us nothing about how much we need from others; it tells us how much we need to grieve the irrevocably barren past and evoke our own inner sources of nurturance.

True/False Self:
Unconditional/Conditional Self

Our True Self, with all its free energy, impulses, feelings, and creativity, may have threatened our parents. They, after all, may have been victimized in their own childhood and never came to terms with it. They taught us how to behave in accord with their fear-laden specifications. Some of this led to legitimate socializing. Some of it was violence to our identity.

We then designed a False Self that met with our parents' approval and maintained our role in the family. We felt that safety was possible only within those boundaries. Such "boundaries" became the long-standing habits and patterns that have been our limitations ever since. They were choices that had an origin in wisdom but now may no longer be serving our best interests. They usually please others but diminish us. Alice Miller writes that "the love I gained with such uphill effort and self-defacement was not meant for me at all but for the me I created to please them."

Once we grieve this loss, we release our hidden inner world of unused and unrevealed qualities and notice how much better we thereby feel about ourselves. We lighten up and may even notice that people love us more.

The fear of revealing the True Self is disguised in these words: "If people really knew me, they would not like me." We can change that *sentence* to read: "I am free enough to want everything I say and do to reveal me as I am. I love being seen as I am."

Relationships in Adulthood

Love happened for each of us in childhood in a different way. For some it meant being taken seriously, for others' attention, physical holding, giving things to us, doing things for us, loyalty, etc. There is no one objective way love can be shown that will fit for everyone. *Love is subjective: each person reads it best in the language in which she learned it.* "We mark with light in the memory the few interviews we have had with souls that made our souls wiser, that spoke what we thought, that told us what we knew, that gave us leave to be what we inly are," says Ralph Waldo Emerson.

As adults we feel genuinely loved when someone creates for us a verisimilitude of that same original love we received long ago. Relationships between adults work best when each partner knows his or her own specific ways of feeling loved and tells the other about it. Then the expression of love can be tailored to the unique needs of each partner. As a result we open ourselves to new ways of feeling loved that expand the old limiting ways.

We can, of course, also be seduced into believing someone loves us authentically when he has only happened upon this same special triggerpoint and has no intention of following through on it in the future.

It is always appropriate to ask for love, but to ask any other adult (including our parents in the present) to meet our primal needs is unfair and unrealistic. Most of us emerge from childhood with conscious and unconscious psychic wounds and emotional unfinished business. What we leave incomplete we are doomed to repeat. The untreated traumas of childhood become the frustrating dramas of adulthood. Our fantasy of the "perfect partner," or our disappointments in a relationship we do not change or leave, or the dramas that keep arising in our relationships reveal our unique unmet primal wounds and needs. We try so hard to get from others what once we missed. What was missed can never be made up for, only mourned and let go of. Only then are we able to relate as adults to adults. As Emerson profoundly observes, "when half gods go, the gods arrive."

Healthy adults are not attracted to the negative excitement of relationships in which people are attempting to use them to work out their own unaddressed childhood conundrums. Ironically, this attempt simply recreates the childhood drama anyway. Only personal inner responsibility and griefwork lets the curtain finally fall.

Our body has memorized childhood scenarios of terror or abuse. But this committing to memory is, ironically, a commitment to secrecy. We cannot now consciously recall or tell what happened. Our automatic cellular reflexes in relationships give us clues and mystify us at the same time. "Why do I pull away when she gets close? Was this kind of closeness dangerous to me long ago? Yet, my mind tells me I always wanted to be loved like this. . . ."

It may take many years and just the right circumstances or person to grant us the liberating opening to know and to tell our story in words. When this happens, the memories come back and we hear ourselves putting them into words for the first time. This profound release initiates us into the heavy and healing ways of griefwork.

The healthy adult can tell the difference between a present conflict with a partner and a restimulation of past unfinished distress. The strong feelings tip her off to the presence of archaic stimuli. She acknowledges openly that the feelings are familiar from the past. She takes responsibility for the severity of her reaction and does not implicate this present person in the tying up of an historical loose end. This is riding the present stress to an original distress and so working on a cause rather than on an effect.

How touching and bewildering is our plight in adult relationships! We are actually trying to hold on and to let go at the same time! We want so fervently to hold on to the love our every cell remembers, the love that goes on consoling. We want so desperately to let go of the hurt that every cell remembers, the hurt that goes on hurting. A working relationship is a crucible in which both of these evolutionary human tasks can be fulfilled. We can be nourished by the love we now receive and work through the pain we once suffered.

The love and the pain of the present are directly connected to the love and the pain of the past. Once we acknowledge the continuity of our condition, we clearly see our personal work. A relationship—especially the first one in adult life—can put us in the best position to do that work. Our partner stimulates the love and the pain and then—optimally—supports us in healthy responses to them. How much we miss when we run from love or from the normal hurts in a life together! We lose contact with our own history and the healing of it. We lose our chance to capitalize on the here and now and so get past the past to live in the unencumbered present.

Mourning and Letting Go

What is at first a cup of sorrow becomes at last immortal wine.
—Gita

Mourning is the appropriate response to loss. It can proceed through these stages, though the order and timing are unique to each person.

I. Reminiscence about any pain, abandonment, perfidy, or abuse we saw and/or felt. This does not have to be a specific memory about what happened. Our bodies remember more reliably than our minds. A *sense* of our deprivation or loss is enough.

II. Full acknowledgement, experiencing, and expression of feelings (e.g. sadness, hurt, anger, fear), so that resolution (catharsis) occurs. For example, tears that demonstrate sadness but do not dissipate it are not useful in the completion of griefwork.

We can express our feelings directly to the people involved, or in therapy, or by ourselves. It is important to say the word goodbye at this time and throughout the process of grieving.

Betrayal, abandonment, rejection, disappointment, humiliation, isolation, etc. are not feelings but beliefs. Each of these judgments keeps us caught in our story and blinded to the bare fact of loss. Each is a subtle form of blame. Each assuages, coddles, and justifies our bruised ego. Each distracts us from the true feelings of grief. Grievances dislocate grief work. Anger without blame completes it.

III. Healing of memories by reexperiencing them with compassion (for our parents and ourselves) and with power, by imagining ourselves speaking up self-protectively to abuse. This includes a sixfold affirmation with the appropriate feelings for each area of grief, separately for each parent.

Here is the paradigm for the healing of memories:

1. Remembering a loss with sadness and anger. *"Loss" includes any specific non-fulfillment of a need or any abuse, humiliation, rejection, or neglect.*

2. Thanks that thereby I began to learn self-reliant ways to compensate for this loss. *Remember and congratulate yourself for some wise maneuver you found to take care of yourself in childhood. Here we acknowledge the gift dimension of the wounds, since betrayal and hurt, though never justifiable, are nonetheless what every human being needs in order to separate and to develop sensitivity, depth, fortitude, self-reliance and empathy. Joseph had to be betrayed by his brothers before he could achieve his wonderful destiny.*

3. Imagining myself speaking up assertively and effectively in childhood. *Picture your household in childhood and a scene of abuse or neglect. Now form an image of yourself acting with full assertiveness and successful self-protection in that same past scene. This is reexperiencing with power and no longer as a victim.*

4. Forgiveness of my parent(s). *Such automatic compassion is the best signal that we have resolved our feelings. Forgiveness can be real only after anger and sadness have been expressed. Paul Tillich says, "Forgiveness is the highest form of forgetting because it is forgetting in spite of remembering."*

5. Dropping the expectation that others fulfill this need for me now.

6. Taking care of this need for myself now as abundantly as I just imagined myself doing in childhood.

Here is an example of the sixfold affirmation to be spoken and written:

- I am and feel sad and angry that my parent(s) failed to stand up for me.
- I am thankful that thereby I began to learn to stand up for myself.
- I imagine speaking up successfully in childhood.
- I forgive my parents for failing to stand up for me.

- I drop the expectation of getting others to stand up for me now (though I appreciate it when they do).
- Now I stand up for myself with full power and effectiveness.

IV. A ritual that shows what we have felt and accomplished in our griefwork. A ritual is any gesture that enacts our intention or commemorates our attainment. An example: Write about the whole process, burn it, and plant a tree or flower together with the ashes while saying "goodbye." Distilling your grief process into one affirmation and burying a copy of it with the ashes is also useful.

V. Getting on with our life, not as victims of the irreversible past, but as adults who have engendered an "inner nurturant parent." Now we are no longer afraid to be kind to ourselves, to treat ourselves to abundance, to stop depriving ourselves, to stop absorbing pain. This self-parenting is the best condition for true intimacy because, like all good parenting, it is a bridge from aloneness to the world of relating. It ends dependency and allows us to relate as equals with our adult partner. Now "need-fulfillment" becomes enrichment. Only those who can take care of themselves are free from the two main obstacles to adult relating: being needy or care-taking others. "I will come to you, my friend, when I no longer need you. Then you will find a palace, not an almshouse," Thoreau once said.

The true healing power of griefwork extends to past *and* present. Each issue to be grieved addresses these two areas of concern: the loss or neglect you experienced in the past, and the lifetime habit that may have sprung from the original hurt.

For example, you grieve how your parents refused to listen to you in childhood. Now in adult life, you notice that you still hide your feelings from most people. This secretiveness may be your lifelong over-reaction to an original injunction from parents who were afraid to know you. Now you are afraid to let others know you.

The past is grieved fully only when the present is healed, too. In fact, the energy that had been tied up in past hurts has finally become available to you for reinvestment in new ways of living. To continue with our example: you now make a choice to reveal more and more about yourself to more and more people. You drop secretiveness and notice that you survive. Some people will reject or betray you for this openness, some will love you more than ever. But their response is secondary because your fear has changed to flexibility. Now you have cleared the wake of a ship that passed long ago, and healed the scarred present with the newfound powers of the healed past.

A Lifelong Work

The above model can be adapted to any area of mourning. Grief work applies to everything we lose or leave. It includes as normal stages: anger, denial (disbelief), bargaining, depression, and acceptance. These are repeated in different sequences over and over throughout our lives, but each time with less debilitating charge and more personal empowerment. Finally only nostalgia remains, a light grief without the painful sadness. At last we contain our own history—no longer driven or possessed by it.

The healthy adult allows hurtful events from his past to become neutral facts by fully grieving the pain and so letting go of them. In this way, one retains the memories but drops the charged, obsessive thoughts of hurt that keep one attached to the drama of it all and vitiate healthy relating. No matter how fully our grief is processed, however, new levels of realization about the loss continually appear. In this sense, grief is truly a lifelong work.

Conclusion

Mourning dismantles the illusions we may have harbored and the secrets we may have kept about our childhood. At first this might have seemed a terrifying prospect. But when it happens in accord with our own timing and in the context of griefwork, it becomes deeply liberating. Once we have allowed ourselves to experience total disillusionment, we will never again know despair.

Mourning is the appropriate response to the loss of what we once had or to the sad realization that we did not have all we needed. We are grieving the *irretrievable* aspect of what we lost and the *irreplaceable* aspect of what we missed. Only these two realizations lead to resolution of grief because only these acknowledge, without denial, how truly bereft we were or are. From the pit of this deep admission that something is irrevocably over and gone, we finally stand clear of the insatiable need to find it again from our parents or partner. To have sought it was to have denied how utter was its absence!

Griefwork done with consciousness builds self-esteem since it shows us our courageous faithfulness to the reality of loss. It authenticates us as adults who can say *Yes* to sadness, anger, and hurt. Such an heroic embrace of our own truth transforms emptiness into capacity. As Jung notes, "your inner emptiness conceals just as great a fullness if you only allow it."

Our psychological work is to journey from the chaos of our personal unconscious to a coherent conscious integration. Our spiritual path then takes us to the treasures of the cosmic (collective) unconscious and full individuation. Everything in our lives, no matter how terrible, exists in relation to an inner healing force. "The journey with father and mother up and down many ladders represents the making conscious of infantile contents that have not yet been integrated. . . . This personal unconscious must always be dealt with first . . . otherwise the gateway to the collective unconscious cannot be opened," Jung tells us.

Our psycho-spiritual work as adults is thus an heroic journey, since a hero is anyone who has lived through pain and been transformed by it. A universal theme in the myths about the early life of the hero is that he is threatened, hurt, or rejected, e.g. Dionysus, Moses, Christ. But "the divine child naturally always escapes. It is the last outbreak of darkness against something already so powerful that although newly born, it cannot be suppressed any more," as Marie-Louise von Franz points out.

> *People whose integrity has not been damaged in childhood, who were protected, respected, and treated with honesty by their parents, will be—both in their youth and adulthood—intelligent, responsive, empathic, and highly sensitive. They will take pleasure in life and will not feel any need to kill or even hurt others or themselves. They will use their power to defend themselves but not to attack others. They will not be able to do otherwise than to respect and protect those weaker than themselves, including their children, because this is what they have learned from their own experience and because it is this knowledge (and not the experience of cruelty) that has been stored up inside them from the beginning. Such people will be incapable of understanding why earlier generations had to build up a gigantic war industry in order to feel at ease and safe in this world. Since it will not have to be their unconscious life-task to ward off intimidation experienced at a very early age, they will be able to deal with attempts at intimidation in their adult life more rationally and more creatively.*

—Alice Miller

2. ASSERTIVENESS SKILLS

For the person who has learned to let go and let be, nothing can ever get in the way again.

—Meister Eckhart

Assertiveness is the personal power to:
—Be clear about your feelings, choices, and agenda
—Ask for what you want
—Take responsibility for your feelings and behavior

Helpful Principles

In each of these principles we see how movement can happen from old habits to new repertories of action. We notice the atavistic ineffective behaviors and leave them behind for creative adult responsibility.

- Early in life, you may have learned that it is not legitimate to:
—Show your real feelings
—Give and receive openly
—Ask for things directly
—Tell your opinions
—Take care of your own interests
—Say No to what you do not want
—Act as if you deserved abundance
    These are injunctions against having power, and to the extent that we have internalized them, we have disabled ourselves and limited our adult capacities. Our journey to wholeness begins from just such a wounded place.

- At first you may believe yourself to be vain, cold, petty, impolite, selfish, or demanding when you act assertively. These disempowering judgments come from an inner critic (usually of early origin). Without attempting to refute or eradicate this voice, simply dub it over by acting as if your wants and needs were worthy. Behavior changes attitudes. Gradually the inner critic is ignored into silence and self-esteem blooms.

- The practice of assertiveness means acting. Act as if you are already the healthiest person you can be. Do not wait until you feel better about yourself or until you believe you have what it takes. Act as if you are self-actualized and your beliefs will follow suit. Act while you fear rather than waiting until you feel unafraid.

  "Acting as if" is a form of playfulness. Play successfully combines contrasts and opposites. When we act as if we are already more advanced than we imagine ourselves to be, we are creatively playing with an old, habitual self-image and welcoming a new self that wants to emerge. This new self is encouraged into existence by the image we are displaying when we "act as if."

- The art in assertiveness is to ask strongly for what you want and then to let go of it if the answer is *No*. You tread the fine line between consistent perseverance and the stubborn persistence that can feel to others like abuse. Passive people do not ask for what they want. Aggressive people demand (openly) or manipulate (secretly) to get what they want. Assertive people simply ask, without inhibition of themselves or pressure on others.

- Your assertiveness may be interpreted by others as aggression. If this happens: adjust your manner to a level that is less threatening; reassure people you love that you are simply asking for what you want, not demanding it; continually acknowledge others' right to say *No* to you. Assertiveness is, after all, "power to" not "power over."

- You do not hurt others' feelings by assertiveness. "Hurt feelings" in others may mean:
  1. you are bullying them, i.e. being aggressive rather than assertive, or
  2. they are not open to interacting with an assertive person, or
  3. the assertiveness has triggered fear or sadness from their own past. "It is such a secret place, the land of tears" (*The Little Prince*).

- Check out your feelings, suspicions, or doubts with the people involved. Whenever possible, check out your decisions with a neutral friend before proceeding to an action. Do this not because you are inadequate, but because you acknowledge your human capacity to overlook something that may be important but only visible to an objective observer.

- It is crucial to remain focused in assertiveness and not to be distracted by argumentativeness. Assertiveness is not a strategy by which you get your way or win victories over others. It is a set of non-violent, non-competitive principles that manifest your values and integrity. The outcome is secondary. Authentic self-presentation is primary.

- You can respond to the negative *impact* of others' behavior toward you while still acknowledging their positive *intention*. Their intention does not excuse their behavior. "I know you mean to help me, but I feel pushed and want to do this in my own time."

- No one creates your feelings. No one is to blame for your situation. You are the author of your condition. Whatever you have been doing is what you are really choosing, whether or not you consciously want it. The alternative is to see yourself as a victim of people or circumstances and real change becomes impossible. Taking responsibility always leads to a revelation of what your next step needs to be.

• Since assertiveness means taking care of yourself, speaking up is not always appropriate. When the other person is out of control, violent, or under the influence of alcohol or drugs, the assertive person makes no attempt to talk sense or make a point. Simply getting away may be the most assertive and intelligent response.

• When you are suddenly threatened or confronted, especially unjustly, you may feel immobilized by fear. In such stress you are less capable of "thinking on your feet." The assertive person asks for time out to collect himself before having to respond. Notice the paradox: (1) I admit fear and vulnerability as a real though temporary disability; (2) I insist on self-restorative time; (3) I act with access to my full power now that I am honoring my own timing.

• Trying without doing is wishing rather than choosing. You either have a plan in place or you are choosing not to act. "This being the case, how shall I proceed?" is a Zen saying that shows the automatic, assertive progression from circumstance to action.

• You can be *informed* by others' behavior rather than *affected* by it. You can observe the behavior of others without having to react to it or to be controlled by it. You operate from your own repertory of responses that uphold you no matter what others do, say, or mean to you.

• You may ask people to understand, hear, and acknowledge your feelings, but you do not need their validation. Your feelings stand on their own merit, and every time you express them you validate yourself. At the same time, you validate others' feelings when you are assertive. You show that you see the legitimacy of what they feel and you understand and care about them for what they feel. This validation is so much more self-empowering than self-defense in which you attempt to discount feelings to avoid facing them or from mistaken guilt about "causing" them.

- Assertiveness makes clarity valuable. As a result you will be quite satisfied after an encounter with someone if you have honestly presented yourself and your position. Your satisfaction will no longer depend upon whether the other person acknowledged you or agreed with you. You will no longer wish you had said more. You will have no need to correct people's impressions of you by going back to say more. "I spoke in accord with the truth accessible to me at that moment and that is enough, even though I might have said it more effectively."

- Assertiveness will feel fearsome and risky. Risk really means "not in control of the outcome." When you are assertive, you stop trying to control circumstances or others' behavior. When you are attached to staying in control, you are betraying the part of yourself that is fearless.

I. Assertiveness: Owning Your Power
THE WAY OF THE HEALTHY EGO
1. Be Clear

Say yes when you mean yes, no when you mean no, and maybe when you mean maybe. (Note that assertiveness means being clear, not necessarily sure.)

Show your feelings, choices, and agenda openly.

Check out your fantasies, doubts, fears, and intuitions with those whom they concern. "Why do we think the face has turned away that only looked elsewhere?" (Erik Erikson).

Tell people it is not acceptable for them to judge, hurt, or blame you.

2. Ask for What You Want

Clear messages from others.

Acknowledgement of your feelings.

Nurturance, appreciation, and constructive criticism.

3. Take Responsibility

Accept others' right to make assertions to you.

Inquire of others about their feelings toward you.

Acknowledge accountability for your feelings.

Finish your emotional unfinished business directly with the people involved or in your own therapy.

Admit your mistakes, oversights, and offenses, and make amends.

II. Passivity: Giving Your Power Away
THE WAY OF THE FEARFUL EGO

Passivity is:

- Refusing to express feelings, act, or decide because of what MIGHT happen to you.
- Making excuses for others' hurtful behavior and not dealing with them about it.
- Over-politeness: always putting others first or letting them take your turn or disturb you without your speaking up.
- Acting from a sense of obligation (a form of fear).
- Smoothing over situations so that the real feelings do not emerge (from yourself or others).
- Over-commitment: doing too much for too long for too little thanks, and when even more is asked of you, doing it dutifully.
- Not registering your recoil from biased remarks or jokes.
- Abandoning yourself by assessing abuse of you from the past or present as justified or "understandable."

- Avoiding decisive action by coping with an unsatisfactory situation or relationship or hoping it might change. WHAT WE ARE NOT CHANGING, WE ARE CHOOSING.

III. Aggressiveness: Changing Power to Control

THE WAY OF THE BELLIGERENT EGO

Aggressiveness is:

- Attempting to control or manipulate others.
- Putting others down by name-calling, insults, or blame. This includes sarcasm, even among friends, or meant in jest.
- Rescuing others: doing for them what they can do for themselves. This victimizes and infantilizes them and gives you dominance over them.
- Emotional or physical violence.
- Competitiveness and attempts to prove people wrong.
- Acting spitefully or vengefully toward people who are rude or hurtful to you.

Basic Rights of the Assertive Person

1. To ask for 100% of what you want from 100% of the people in your life, 100% of the time.

2. To enjoy emotional and physical safety. No one has the right to hurt you, even if she loves you.

3. To change your mind or to make mistakes.

4. To decide when and whether or not you are responsible for (a) finding solutions to others' problems or
(b) taking care of their needs.

5. To say No or Maybe without pressure to decide in accord with someone else's timing.

6. To be illogical in making decisions.

7. To have secrets, to decide how much of yourself or your life you choose to reveal.

8. To be free to explain your choices or not (includes not having to make excuses or give reasons when you say No).

9. To be non-assertive when you see that as appropriate.

10. To maintain the same principles, skills, and rights of assertiveness with your partner, parents, children, or friends.

SUMMARIZING ASSERTIVENESS

Assertiveness is affirming your own truth and receiving others' truth:

You ask for what you want and honor the response.

You share what you feel and accept what others feel.

You really are responsible, so you act that way and you ask the same from others.

Practicing assertiveness leads to a realization that you have alternatives, no matter how confining your predicament may be.

The experience of choice combined with support from others offers the best conditions for departure from the depressing sense of yourself as a victim. Instead, you get on with your life in a powerful, adult, and confident way.

Like one who lives in a valley and then crosses the mountains and sees the plain, he knows now from experience that the sign saying "Do not go beyond this point," like the high mountains, does not signify a barrier.

—Alice Miller

The achievement of assertiveness requires that we come to terms with three crucial issues that confront everyone: fear, anger, and guilt. These challenges to mature adulthood are treated in the next three chapters which complete our exploration of assertiveness.

3. FEAR:
CHALLENGE TO ADULTHOOD I

The certainty that nothing can happen to us that does not in our innermost being belong to us is the foundation of fearlessness.

—Govinda

Definitions

Fear is the feeling that arises in response to present danger. It is a No to what seems unabsorbable. Like all feelings, fear is based on a subjective belief that a certain stimulus poses a threat.

Appropriate fear leads to a flight or fight response which is activated and dealt with, and is followed by repose. This fear is necessary since it signals a danger we need to avoid or eliminate.

Neurotic fear engages the flight/fight pattern but never follows through on it. This can be simply good sense for smooth living in society or it can be a personal block and thus self-limiting.

Neurotic fear shows us what we have failed to integrate. For example, fear of the water vanishes by learning to swim. Swimming is, in effect, how water (subjective threat) is integrated. We have adapted to a former danger, befriended it, and become comfortable with it through skill and knowledge. We now approach the water with consciousness and competence, the components that signal integration. Moreover, we feel the excitement of the water and all the fun it offers. Less fear has led to more contact with our own liveliness.

Fear is the opposite of love because it is totally conditional. It keeps us out of the water; it excludes. Love is all-inclusive. To say that "love casts out fear" is to say that unconditional and conscious integration has triumphed over ignorance and inhibition.

Actually, every problem is something we are having trouble integrating. This tells us that fear is somewhere at the bottom of every obstacle we face. Locating the fear element helps us work through it with more consciousness.

Negative Excitement

Neurotic fear is unintegrated excitement. The energy in fear is simply blocked excitement that can be released by wholehearted, active engagement with the realities that threaten us. How this can be done is the final subject of this chapter.

Negative excitement is a stressful form of pain in which we fear and desire the same object at the same time. It is an addictive energy that usually stems from old emotional business that has been activated by the dramatic complications in our life story.

Negative excitement can keep us stuck for years in dysfunctional, abusive, or self-defeating circumstances. It sometimes feels like a sense of purpose since it sustains our ongoing drama. When the object of our negative excitement is gone, we may then feel depressed and even believe our life has lost meaning.

The best way to handle negative excitement is to treat it as an addiction and work a twelve step program of recovery, e.g. Co-dependents Anonymous.

Rationalization

Every fear and addiction is upheld and maintained by rationalizations, reasons used to prevent change. "I am afraid to reach out because I might be rejected." This fear has no *real* object, only a possible one, but the given reason (rationalization) maintains a stalemate and the person remains afraid.

Here are three ways in which rationalizations maintain fear:

1. The "reason" is meant to keep us in control by protecting us from surprises. This control backfires by vitiating our own resilience, a prerequisite for the integration of fear.

2. The "reason" blockades access to adult solutions. We are so attached to a long-held belief that we lose perspective and mobility for change.

3. The "reason" directly maintains the inertia of fear since we go on fearing what we refuse to confront.

The irony in all three of these is that what is meant to protect us *from* fear only protects the fear itself. Rationalization is the sentry that guards not us but the fear in us!

Fear of Other People

What is happening when certain people scare us?

1. We may be afraid of the uncontrollable feelings that a certain person evokes in us. *If you fear someone you can trust with your feelings, admit your fear and its basis to him directly.* "I'm afraid that you won't approve of me and that I will feel hurt when I'm rejected." *You may paradoxically lighten the process by exaggerating:* "I'm afraid that if you reject me, I'll die!"

Making these admissions aloud every time you feel the fear shows its humorous dimension and its highly subjective origin. Gradually, the fear steps back in embarrassment!

If you fear someone you cannot trust, change your situation by leaving it or handling the fear within your own support system (friends, therapy, etc.) It takes courage to admit your limits and not damage yourself by staying in no-win stress and pain. Endurance of such humiliation erodes self-esteem and keeps you afraid.

2. The *other* person may be afraid and we are picking up on the fear she is projecting. She may, for instance, fear closeness and use an intimidating manner to safeguard distance. *If you suspect that someone fears you but is not admitting it, dispel the secrecy by asking directly about the fear.* "Are you afraid I might get too close? I do not

want to do that. Let's talk about the amount of closeness you want to receive and the amount I want to give."

3. Specific people, through unconscious or conscious clues, elicit old parental or childhood terrors. This is especially true when we seem helpless or when we feel too afraid even to defend ourselves. *Explore your fears to find their origin. If they are kindled by your early life, do the griefwork that can heal the scared child within as described in Chapter 1.*

4. Some people reflect back to us our own Shadow side. We configure others to be "greater than" us, positively by awe, and negatively by dread. Actually, we are fearing the admirable or despicable qualities unintegrated in ourselves. *If they are Shadow fears, use the guidelines in Chapter 10 to work with them. Then you take responsibility for your fears, and this gesture can lead to a breakthrough for you.*

Working on Neurotic Fears

Admit your fear to yourself, to the person involved and/or to any person you trust. Admitting cuts through denial and attends to reality. This attention releases the healing and power that we have refused to claim or employ.

Allow the feeling of fear fully with no attempt to suppress it or to be free of it.

Acting because of fear is cowardice; **acting** *with* fear is the courage that survives it.

   Techniques helpful in the process of "acting as if" are:
   a) Take deep breaths from the diaphragm (since anxious breathing is thoracic).
   b) Focus on an image that increases serenity.
   c) Ask for support from a friend or ask for inner support by imaging a strong person who accompanies you as a guide or coach.

Results

The "triple A approach" in working through fear is an unconditional engagement with what is. We are reversing our No to what seemed unabsorbable to a Yes to what is integratable.

We thus make contact with our own liveliness, the positive excitement which had been blocked by fear. The energy that went into elaborate fictions, defenses, and rationalizations is reinvested in personal power and freedom from fear. "I am powerless in the face of this fear" changes to "I found a choice where I thought there was only a dead end."

The demon power of fear is, after all, exactly this apparent choicelessness. Acting *with* fear, i.e. including it, locates and affirms an alternative. The spell is thus broken by what cast the spell! The key was in the lock all the time! Nothing has to go on scaring us. Every human experience is assimilable. This is a foundation of optimism.

Integration is the primary result of working on fear. Chapter 9 provides a detailed explanation of this process. Once a fear is worked through, it releases its liveliness and makes us happier. Notice the paradox of human unfolding: every fear blocks a capacity; every integration of fear reveals and accesses a capacity.

Fear	Integration
Loss	Letting go of attachment
Change	Adjustment
Self-revelation	Self-acceptance
Loneliness	Support system
Intimacy	Commitment
Power	Assertiveness
Feelings	Acceptance of vulnerability

The Void	Staying with it
Failure	Letting the chips fall where they may
Success	Self-esteem

When this ultimate crisis comes . . . when there is no way out—that is the very moment when we explode from within and the totally other emerges: the sudden surfacing of a strength, a security of unknown origin, welling up from beyond reason, rational expectation, and hope.

—Emil Durkheim

4. ANGER:
CHALLENGE TO ADULTHOOD II

Relate to a life situation in the deepest sense: not from the standpoint of the ego that bemoans its fate and rebels against it, but from . . . the greater inner law that has left behind its small birth, the narrow realm of personal outlook, for the sake of renewal and rebirth.

—Max Zeller

Definition

Anger is a natural human feeling that everyone experiences often and that needs to be expressed to maintain psychological health. Anger is the feeling that says No to opposition, injury, or injustice. It is a signal that something I value is in jeopardy.

The physical energy of anger comes from the "fight" side of the flight/fight response of adrenalin.

The psychological energy of anger comes from the real or imagined sense of threat. Anger is thus legitimately expressed even when its foundation is irrational. We express a feeling because it is real for us, not because it has objective justification.

Anger is expressed actively when we show it directly. Usually this involves the raising of one's voice, changes in facial expression and gestures, and a show of excitement and displeasure.

Anger can also be expressed passively, i.e. passive aggressively. One punishes the other without admitting one's anger, e.g. tardiness, gossip, silence, refusal to cooperate, absence, rejection, malice to cause pain, etc. Passive anger is inappropriate and not an adult way of behaving. Strongly expressed anger is called rage. Strongly held anger is called hate. Unexpressed anger is resentment. Anger can be unconsciously repressed and internalized. It then becomes depression, i.e. anger turned inward.

When anger is consciously suppressed, we choose not to know or show it. The motivation is usually fear but we seldom acknowledge the fear. Instead we rationalize the suppression as politeness or social amenity, configuring the expression of anger as unnecessary.

Fear of Anger

Why do we feel so unsafe about expressing anger openly? We may have found early in life that showing anger was dangerous. There are two main ways to have learned this:

1) Showing anger in our childhood may have meant no longer being loved or approved and now we are acting as if that were still true. Processing such archaic equations may lead to the liberating realization that anger and love coexist in authentic intimacy. Anger, like any true feeling, cannot affect, mar, or cancel real love.

Anger is inevitable in any relationship in which people are free and in which they allow one another to get close. "To let ourselves be touched also involves letting ourselves be scraped," writes John Welwood. Love without the safety to allow anger is not love but fear. When adults love they reveal their own anger and welcome it from others. This is a way in which the truth sets us free!

2) Receiving anger may seem dangerous because previously in life anger has led to violence, either physically or emotionally. But this was not real anger, only a dramatic mime of it. Anger does not lead to danger, distance, or violence. Drama does. In this context, drama means ego-centered, manipulative theatrics with an explanatory storyline attached. Many of us have never seen real anger, only drama.

Drama and Anger

We distinguish anger (a true feeling) from drama (an avoidance of true feeling). It takes heroic work to drop drama and show responsible anger. The neurotic ego clings to negative excitement. The adult functional ego loves the positive excitement of expressing true feeling and then being released from it.

DRAMA	TRUE ANGER
Scares the hearer	Informs the hearer and creates attention in the hearer
Is meant to silence the other	Is meant to communicate with the other
Masks the dashed expectation or fear of not being in control with a false sense of control	Contains sadness or disappointment and these are acknowledged
Blames the other for what one feels	Takes responsibility for this feeling as one's own
Is a strategy that masks a demand that the other change	Asks for change but allows the other to change or not
Is violent, aggressive, out of control, derisive, punitive	Is nonviolent, always in control and within safe limits
Represses the true feeling	Expresses an assertive response
Occludes other feelings	Coexists with other feelings
Creates stress because one's bruised, scared ego is impotently enraged	Releases the aliveness in one's true self
Is held on to and endures as resentment	Is brief and then let go of with a sense of closure
Insists the other see how justified one is	Needs no response

Applying this distinction to the experience of rejection, notice the difference in reactions:

Drama is a belligerent reaction to rejection that punishes by further distancing	Anger is an intimate response to rejection that bridges the distance or allows it without long-held resentment
Drama is based on indignation that one was not treated with the love and loyalty one unconsciously believes one is entitled to	Anger is based on displeasure at what happened but with consciousness that this feeling is based on a subjective interpretation

---

It is often said that anger is a "secondary feeling," one that masks another feeling, such as sadness or fear. Notice that anger, like all feelings, *coexists* with other feelings. It never masks them. Drama does that. Where else would masks fit so well?

"Holding onto anger" is also impossible since anger is the shortest feeling. It cannot be held onto. Once it is expressed fully, relief and letting go follow automatically. What is held onto is not anger but a set of storylines that keep the drama ignited.

Anger and Belief

Anger, like all feelings, is not caused by an event but by our belief about or interpretation of an event.

Here is a paradigm, based on the work of Albert Ellis, that elucidates this process:

An Action occurs (open to any interpretation)

My Belief interprets the action in a specific way

A Consequence occurs: the feeling based on the belief that was triggered by the action

So **A:** What happened
  B: What I believe
  C: What I feel

It may seem that **A** led to **C**. But **B**, the disappeared middle, requires attention. **A** can only get to **C** through **B**!

In this psychological chain, one stimulus does not cause another. **A** does not cause **B** or **C**. **B** does not cause **C**. **A** triggers **B** and **B** triggers **C**.

This explains why we are responsible for our own feelings. Others triggered us by their actions but the interpretation was our own. The consequent feeling was not caused by others' behavior, only occasioned by it. They are accountable for setting a process in motion but not for the final feeling. That is our responsibility alone.

Working on Anger

Using the paradigm above, identify an instance in which you were angry. Then acknowledge (A) the stimulating event and (C) your anger. Now admit: my feeling (C) about his behavior (A) would not have arisen unless I believed (B).

Here is an example:

A: You did not keep your promise.
C: I became angry.
B: I believe I am entitled to be treated fairly.
  I expected you to be honest.
  I believe I was insulted by this betrayal.

You have now identified at least four beliefs behind your interpretation of the broken promise: entitlement, expectation, betrayal, and insult. Now match these beliefs against your own history, especially in childhood. Were you betrayed before? Were the betrayals, abandonments, and abuses of early life ever mourned and processed? If they were not, they remain raw and distressed now. The beliefs and anger are signals of unfinished emotional business. This event has reopened old wounds. Now you begin to see how much of your reaction to this present stimulus is your own business. *The anger has pointed to where it still hurts.*

Finally, entitlement, expectation, and insult are neurotic ego issues. Adults who are building more functional ego responses see through the power of such dramatic cues. They let go of entitlement by asking for what they want while acknowledging that sometimes people come through and sometimes they do not. They drop expectations (one-sided) and ask for agreements (two-sided). They ask for amends when they are insulted and shun those who consistently refuse to treat them respectfully.

Parsing an anger experience has led to more understanding of myself, more clarity about where my work is, and more responsibility for my own reactions. Now I am not thinking of myself as a victim. I have grown in assertiveness and self-esteem while still validating my anger as legitimate. Anger is still real even when its origins are in childish or atavistic beliefs.

Affirming Anger

1. I accept anger as healthy and I examine the belief behind it and the personal history it evokes.

2. I take responsibility for the feeling as legitimate and as totally mine.

3. I express my anger but I choose not to act out aggressively by retaliation, vindictiveness, or malice.

4. I embrace more adult beliefs about myself and the world so that my anger now arises from an informed sense of justice without the "insulted, arrogant ego" dimension.

Lively Energy

Anger is fresh lively energy that is valuable to our individual evolution. We use our anger to break the stranglehold of ego and fear. We follow our anger to the sources of our own hitherto unfranchised psychic territory. The anger stimulates our power. It is not something we need to drop or deny. It is something that lifts us and transforms us once we allow ourselves to feel it and show it.

> In the intensity of the emotional turbulence itself lies the value, the energy . . . to remedy the problem.
>
> —Jung

5. GUILT:
CHALLENGE TO ADULTHOOD III

All self-knowledge is purchased at the cost of guilt.
—Paul Tillich

Appropriate Guilt and My Truth

Appropriate guilt precedes or follows unethical behavior. It flows from an internal organismic resonance (conscience) that evaluates action in accord with personal conviction. "We are born with an inherent bodily wisdom which helps us distinguish experiences that actualize or do not actualize our potential," says Carl Rogers. This is our functional ego telling us when we have stepped out of our own truth. This guilt indicates a rending of our integrity or an upsetting of a natural balance between ourselves and others. The balance is restored by admission and restitution.

Neurotic Guilt and Their Truth

Neurotic guilt is a learned (non-organismic) response to an external injunction or demand that we have internalized. We have stepped out of others' truth. This guilt is not let go of by amends and restitution but hangs on. Its origin is in the neurotic ego and it leads to an inner conflict, not to balance.

Guilt is not a feeling but a belief or judgment. Appropriate guilt is a judgment that is self-confronting and leads to resolution. Neurotic guilt is a judgment that is self-defeating and leads to unproductive pain. Appropriate guilt is resolved in reconciliation and restitution. Neurotic guilt seeks to be resolved by punishment. In appropriate guilt there is accountability. In neurotic guilt there is blame. In short, appropriate guilt is an adult response; neurotic guilt is the response of a scared child within us.

Guilt Tricks

In every experience of neurotic guilt, there is something we are refusing to acknowledge. This guilt is a tactic we use to avoid feelings and truths:

1. A Disguise for Fear

Guilt that holds us back from acting can be a disguise for the fear of assertiveness. Guilt that follows a strong choice can be a fear of loss of love or of approval. We may fear the consequences of not being liked or of our losing control when we have strayed too far from an inhibition. The prior guilt can paralyze us and we then remain stuck or passive. The consequent guilt makes us ashamed and frightened of reprisals or of being known (or of knowing ourselves) in a new way.

2. A Downplay of Responsibility

Neurotic guilt limits us to one single course of legitimate behavior. In this respect, guilt inhibits imagination, the creative basis of choice. As long as we are caught in guilt, we do not see possibilites or know what we really want. This is how guilt subverts assertiveness.

Guilt after acting or after the omission of an act can also be a way of minimizing the power of the choice we have made. We are less responsible if we judge ourselves guilty because then our whole self was not committed! Paradoxically, guilt thus lets us off the hook and creates a false sense of righteousness.

3. A Mask for Anger

Guilt can mean justifiable anger toward a respected parent, authority figure, or friend who seems to have obligated or inhibited us. We believe it is unsafe or wrong to feel or to express this anger. This leaves only us to be wrong and so the unexpressed anger turns inward as guilt. Thus guilt lets others off the hook while we abuse ourselves with anger that was meant for them.

4. A Dodge of Truth

Guilt is sometimes used to avoid an unacceptable truth. For example, during childhood, rather than face the painful truth that my parents did not love me, I believed myself to be guilty of not measuring up to their expectations. Then their lack of love became all my fault. "They had the love stored up for me, but I could not merit its release." Guilt about my own "inadequate behavior" kept the truth about them a secret. What I do not know, even now, I never have to face or get past. In this way guilt keeps me in others' power, i.e. always trying to please them. People-pleasing and a sense of inadequacy grow from this same pillaged wilderness of self-doubt.

Working with Guilt: Moving Toward Health

NEUROTIC

It is impossible to eliminate neurotic guilt entirely. Allow this guilt to be in your mind but no longer let it lead you to act or not to act. Make choices *with* guilt, not because of it. Simply notice what your guilt may be covering up. Is it a mask for fear, refusal to take responsibility, anger, denial of a truth, etc.? Then each time you experience neurotic guilt you acknowledge it as a signal of some avoidance. The guilt then dissipates enough so that you can address the authentic excitement and feeling underlying it. The guilt becomes what it always was: a concept not a precept, a belief not a verdict, a thought not a reality.

Fear is blocked excitement; anger is ignited excitement; guilt is mistaken excitement.

APPROPRIATE

It is unnecessary and dangerous to eliminate appropriate guilt. Appropriate guilt helps us know when we have disturbed a moral balance. Unlike neurotic guilt which hangs on, appropriate guilt vanishes automatically with a program of admission, amends, and affirmation. Work through appropriate guilt with this "Triple A" approach:

1. Admission

Admit directly to the person involved that you hurt him or acted irresponsibly or neglectfully. Ask to hear about the pain he feels and listen to it. Thereby you live through the pain and become fully conscious of your behavior and its consequences. This is a powerful way finally to take full responsibility for your actions. In this process, genuine intimacy becomes possible in relationships.

2. Amendment

Make amends in two ways: first, cease the behavior; second, make restitution directly or to a charity or to a substitute person if the original person is unavailable or unready for your amendment. Amendment is authentic when it includes a dedication to change the behavior for the future. Remorse is sorrow without amendment. It lowers self-esteem and prevents release from guilt.

3. Affirmation

Affirmation following this guilt-work takes two forms:

First, use any of the affirmations at the end of this book that resonate for you personally. Designing your own affirmations is even more useful.

Second, affirm (congratulate) yourself for the adult choice and the follow-through that made the guilt process ultimately empowering.

As a result of these three steps, a spiritual shift may occur: you become compassionate toward yourself and others. Now, instead of an immediate recrimination, you notice the connection between present unacceptable behavior and past or early learning. In other words, you see yourself (and others) in the context of compassionate understanding.

You then hold yourself *accountable* but not to *blame*. Blame leads to an emotionally-charged self-repudiation. Accountability leads to matter-of-fact amendment and higher self-esteem. By compassion and accountability, we affirm a self-forgiveness, the authentic and final name for self-actualization. "That by which we fall is that by which we rise" (Tantric saying).

> By noon, the island had gone down in the horizon; and all before us was the wide Pacific.
>
> —Herman Melville: Omoo

6. VALUES AND SELF-ESTEEM

These roses under my window make no reference to former roses or to better ones; they are for what they are . . . there is no time for them. There is simply the rose; it is perfect in every moment of its existence.

—Ralph Waldo Emerson

A psychologically and spiritually conscious person acts from a consistent—though always evolving—sense of values. To value is to esteem the worth of something, to declare that it has meaning for us.

Characteristics of Values

1. Values are organismic, i.e. they arise from within you in a natural way. A set of values is not imposed from without. It is a province of your inner world. A sense of values is really a sense of your own identity. You are thus esteeming and trusting yourself.

2. Your values have been consciously chosen from a variety of alternatives. To know your values is to know yourself, since your choices reveal you.

3. Your values are revealed to others by your words and actions. Your behavior is the final determinant of your values. This is how people come to trust you: they can see your consistency. You act on your inner choices.

4. As your values become more and more conscious, you are more and more apt to proclaim them—even at great cost to your own comfort and ambitions. People may respect this integrity and admire or appreciate you. This gratifies you though it does not motivate you.

5. Those deep-seated, usually long-held, inflexible beliefs

(hold-outs) about how the world or you or others should be are based on rigid judgments and archaic fears, not on values. Such ulterior inflexibility keeps you unfree and prevents your full self-emergence. It kills spontaneity, permeability, and finally compassion. "Non-ambiguity and non-contradiction are too one-sided to express the incomprehensible," Jung observes.

Our aliveness is our capacity to give and receive. Intransigence and sanctimony slam the door in the face of such a generous guest. "Judgment and closure are the greatest dangers to one who wants to retain the psychic mobility of an explorer," John Lilly once wrote.

Personal Values and Identity

Our personal values identify us to ourselves and others. In a very real way, we are the values we cherish and demonstrate.

To act out of the fear of guilt or of looking bad or of punishment means that our values have not had the chance to achieve their full primacy in our lives. We consequently feel "unworthy." Our self-esteem diminishes because our actions emanate from guilt or from fear of how others may estimate us.

Having values, however, does not mean that our actions and motives are pure. The conscious adult has the ability to contain apparently contradictory motivations. It is unrealistic to expect that an altruistic decision will not contain some selfish motivation or that a generous decision will not contain some element of sanctimony or of a sense of obligation. The negative element in no way vitiates the positive element. They coexist as shadows coexist with light. The adult concern is only with the ratio. "This time I bring one more moment of pure care about you than I had last time."

Awakening Values

To awaken values that are undeveloped or have become dormant, we can follow these guidelines:

1. Trust intuitions, the inner messages that tell us what is to be honored and what is to be avoided.

2. Notice how many choices you make to feel good and make more choices to feel good about yourself.

3. Check out motivations and choices with a person or community or program whose integrity you trust. Then make your own decisions, now more objectively informed.

4. Notice which values you admire stongly in others. Act in accord with the values you admire while acknowledging that guilt may also partially motivate you.

5. Gradually, a shift occurs and the guilt-motivation decreases as the value-motivation increases. Acting on values becomes easeful and you love yourself more. Then self-esteem flourishes and self-deprecation dies away.

Not to be attached to something is to be aware of its infinite value.

—Shunryu Suzuki

SUMMARY REFLECTIONS ON PART ONE: DECLARATIONS OF A HEALTHY ADULTHOOD

Will it not call for the whole duration of centuries before our sight is attuned to the light? . . . I am prepared to press on to the end along a path on which each step makes me more certain, toward horizons that are ever more shrouded in mist.
—Teilhard de Chardin

I accept full responsibility for the shape my life has taken.

I need never fear my own truth, powers, fantasies, wishes, thoughts, sexuality, dreams, or ghosts.

I trust that "darkness and upheaval always precede an expansion of consciousness" (Jung).

I let people go away or stay and am still okay.

I accept that I may never feel I am receiving—or have received—all the attention I seek.

I acknowledge that reality is not obligated to me; it remains unaffected by my wishes or rights.

One by one, I drop every expectation of people and things.

I reconcile myself to the limits on others' giving to me and on my giving to them.

Until I see another's behavior with compassion, I have not understood it.

I let go of blame, regret, vengeance, and the infantile desire to punish those who hurt or reject me.

When change and growth scare me, I still choose them. I may act with fear, but never because of it.

I am still safe when I cease following the rules my parents (or others) set for me.

I cherish my own integrity and do not use it as a yardstick for anyone else's behavior.

I am free to have and entertain any thought. I do not have the right to do whatever I want. I respect the limits of freedom and still act freely.

I overcome the urge to retreat on the brink of discovery.

No one can or needs to bail me out. I am not entitled to be taken care of by anyone or anything.

I give without demanding appreciation though I may always ask for it.

I reject whining and complaining as useless distractions from direct action on or withdrawal from unacceptable situations.

I let go of control without losing control.

Choices and perceptions in my life are flexible, not rigid or absolute.

If people knew me as I really am, they would love me for being human like them.

I drop poses and let my every word and deed reveal what I am really like.

Changes and transitions are more graceful as I cooperate with them.

Every human power is accessible to me.

I live by personal standards and at the same time—in self-forgive-ness—I make allowances for my occasional lapses.

I grant myself a margin of error in my work and relationships. I release myself from the pain of having to be right or compe-tent all the time.

I accept that it is normal to feel that I do not always measure up.

I am ultimately adequate to any challenge that comes to me.

My self-acceptance is not complacency since in itself it represents an enormous change.

I am happy as I do what I love and love what is.

Wholehearted engagement with my circumstances releases my irre-pressible liveliness.

I love unconditionally and set sane conditions on my self-giving.

> *The great change never does occur, only matches struck unexpectedly in the dark. Here was one.*
> —Virginia Woolf

part two

Relationship Issues

7. MAINTAINING PERSONAL BOUNDARIES IN RELATIONSHIPS

Your personal boundaries protect the inner core
of your identity and your right to choices:
"There lives the dearest freshness deep-down things."
—Gerard Manley Hopkins

Our journey began at birth with no sense of boundaries. We did not know where mother ended and we began. We felt omnipotently in control of our need fulfillment and of its source.

Our first growthful realization was of separateness. Our first task was letting go, i.e. acknowledging a personal boundary: I am separate and so are those who care about me. This was a departure and a struggle.

It may have felt like an abandonment. From the very beginning of life, we may have equated letting go of attachment with loss of power and of secure need fulfillment.

The mystery of why we hold on so fiercely today may be in this original terrifying and illusory equation.

Adults learn that separateness is not an abandonment but simply a human condition, the only condition from which a healthy relationship can grow.

With boundaries comes interdependence rather than dependency. With boundaries comes personal accountability, not entitlement to be taken care of unilaterally. From boundaries comes the mutuality that drops control of another in favor of honor of another.

Boundaries do not create alienation; they safeguard contiguity. Boundaries are what makes it possible for us to have closeness while we still safely maintain a personal identity.

To give up personal boundaries would mean abandoning ourselves! No relationship can thrive when one or both partners have forsaken the inner unique core of their own separate identity. Love happens when two liberties embrace, salute, and foster one another.

In a healthy person, loyalty has its limits and unconditional love can coexist with conditional involvement. Unconditional does not, after all, mean uncritical. You can both love someone unconditionally and place conditions on your interactions to protect your own boundaries. "I love you unconditionally and I take care of myself by not living with you." This is shrewd fondness!

The essential inner core of yourself must remain intact as relationships begin, change, or end. The journey never violates our wholeness. When you are clear about your personal boundaries, the innate identity that is you is not bestowed by others nor do you let it be plundered by them.

It is building a functional healthy ego to relate intimately to others with full and generous openness while your own wholeness still remains inviolate. It is a great boost to self-esteem to be in-touch *and* intact. This is adult interdependence.

In every truly intimate relationship, we become ego-invested in the other person. This means that we care deeply about our partner's welfare. It also means that we care about our partner's opinions and treatment of us. We are vulnerable to hurt and rejection. We have given power to our partner. This is perfectly normal and flows logically from the nature of commitment.

In a *functional ego investment*, we will give power without thereby being personally diminished. We are vulnerable as lovers not as victims. In other words, our commitment does not mean losing our boundaries.

In a *neurotic ego investment*, we lose our ability to protect ourselves. The actions of our partner then determine our state of mind, rather than simply affect it temporarily. We live by reacting, rather than by taking action.

This is an example of how the unfinished business of early life, discussed in Chapter One, can sabotage adult self-esteem. Those who were abused in childhood *and had no way of defending themselves,* have the most trouble in making a healthy ego-investment in relationships. For them, boundaries were never clear or safe and the drama of relating depletes their tentative ego supplies. Grieving past abuse replenishes the inner silo.

I know I have lost my boundaries and
become co-dependent* when:

"I don't let go of what doesn't work"

and it feels like

"I can't let go of what could work."

Co-dependency is unconditional love for someone else
that has turned against oneself.

Note: The left column of the checklist at the end of this chapter provides a
working definition of "co-dependency."

How to maintain your personal boundaries:

1. Ask directly for what you want. This declares your identity to others and to yourself. The assertiveness skills in Chapter 2 describe clear boundaries, the only conditions for true human freedom. If your boundaries are rigid so that you avoid closeness, you may be in the grip of fear. If your boundaries are loose or undefined, you may be in the lap of submission to others' control.

2. Foster inner self-nurturance (a good parent within oneself). This builds an inner intuitive sense that lets you know when a relationship has become hurtful, abusive, or invasive. It is built as a result of the work you do on your childhood issues (see Chapter 1). It needs the ongoing support of honest feedback from friends, self-help programs, or therapy in order to be maintained.

3. Observe others' behavior toward you—taking it as infor-

mation—without getting caught in their drama. Be a fair witness who sees from a self-protected place. This is honoring your own boundaries. It empowers you then to decide—uninfluenced by another's seductive or aggressive power—how much you will accept of what someone offers you or of what someone fires at you.

4. Maintain a bottom line: a limit to how many times you allow someone to say no, lie, disappoint, or betray you before you will admit the painful reality and move on to mutual work or separate tables. This includes confronting addiction to exciting but futureless relationships in which you keep looking for more where there is only less, keep looking for happiness where there is only hurt. In addiction, our illusory belief compensates for and inflates the diminished reality.

5. Change the locus of trust from others to oneself. As an adult you are not looking for someone you can trust absolutely. You acknowledge the margins of human failing and let go of expecting security. You then trust *yourself* to be able to receive love and handle hurt, to receive trustworthiness and handle betrayal, to receive intimacy and handle rejection.

A Checklist on Boundaries in Relationship

When you give up your boundaries in a relationship you:

1. Are unclear about your preferences

2. Do not notice unhappiness since enduring is your concern

3. Alter your behavior, plans, or opinions to fit the current moods or circumstances of another (live reactively)

4. Do more and more for less and less

5. Take as truth the most recent opinion you have heard

6. Live hopefully while wishing and waiting

7. Are satisfied if you are coping and surviving

8. Let the other's minimal improvement maintain your stalemate

9. Have few hobbies because you have no attention span for self-directed activity

When your boundaries are intact in a relationship you:

1. Have clear preferences and act on them

2. Recognize when you are happy/unhappy

3. Acknowledge moods and circumstances around you while remaining centered (live actively)

4. Do more when that gets results

5. Trust your own intuition while being open to others' opinions

6. Live optimistically while co-working on change

7. Are only satisfied if you are thriving

8. Are encouraged by sincere ongoing change for the better

9. Have excited interest in self-enhancing hobbies and projects

When you give up your boundaries in a relationship you:	*When your boundaries are intact in a relationship you:*
10. Make exceptions for this person for things you would not tolerate in anyone else and accept alibis	10. Have a personal standard that, albeit flexible, applies to everyone and ask for accountability
11. Are manipulated by flattery so that you lose objectivity	11. Appreciate feedback and can distinguish it from attempts to manipulate
12. Keep trying to create intimacy with a narcissist	12. Relate only to partners with whom *mutual* love is possible
13. Are so strongly affected by another that obsession results	13. Are strongly affected by your partner's behavior and take it as information
14. Will forsake every personal limit to get sex or the promise of it	14. Integrate sex so that you can enjoy it but never at the cost of your integrity
15. See your partner as causing your excitement	15. See your partner as stimulating your excitement
16. Feel hurt and victimized but not angry	16. Let yourself feel anger, say "Ouch!" and embark on a program of change
17. Act out of compliance and compromise	17. Act out of agreement and negotiation
18. Do favors that you inwardly resist (cannot say No)	18. Only do favors you choose to do (can say No)
19. Disregard intuition in favor of wishes	19. Honor intuitions and distinguish them from wishes

When you give up your boundaries in a relationship you:

20. Allow your partner to abuse your children or friends

21. Mostly feel afraid and confused

22. Are enmeshed in a drama that unfolds beyond your control

23. Are living a life that is not yours, and that seems unalterable

24. Commit yourself for as long as the other needs you to be committed that way (no bottom line)

25. Believe you have no right to secrets

These entries define "co-dependency."

When your boundaries are intact in a relationship you:

20. Insist others' boundaries be as safe as your own

21. Mostly feel secure and clear

22. Are always aware of choices

23. Are living a life that mostly approximates what you always wanted for yourself

24. Decide how, to what extent, and how long you will be committed

25. Protect your private matters without having to lie or be surreptitious

These entries define "self-parenting."

A helpful way of using this and every chart in this book is to draw a line for every entry with a point at each end (using a separate sheet of paper).

Plot your behavior at an end or center and notice where the majority of your responses fall. They may differ for each person in your life, e.g. poor boundaries with spouse, clear boundaries with parents, moderate boundaries with children.

All of this is information about where your struggle is, where your work needs to be, and where things are satisfactory.

8. INTIMACY

Mutual loving closeness in a committed relationship

I. Elements of True Intimacy

What we are able to offer once our ego is healthy:

1. An abundant inner source of self-nurturance so that we are not desperately needy for someone to depend on (as a child on a parent) or for someone to take care of (as a parent of a child).

2. Trust in ourselves to receive loyalty and handle betrayal. Adult relationships are not based on implicit trust (as parent-child relationships are) but on unconditional love which acknowledges human mutability.

3. The ability to give and to receive. "I get past my fears long enough to disclose my feelings and receive yours, to show affection—both sexually and non-sexually—and to receive yours."

4. Respect for ground rules regarding lifestyles, responsibilities, sex, and differing time/space needs.

5. Encouraging, fearless, and pleased acceptance of the other's unique needs, differences, development, and path.

6. An engaged focus on the other so that one genuinely listens to the other's feelings and concerns without the immediate need to tell one's own story.

7. A commitment to maintain the relationship during periods when one's needs are not being met, since the other is valued for one's inherent worth, not just for need fulfillment.

8. An ability to tolerate love and anger at the same time. "You can be angry at me and I will still love you. When I am angry at you, I still love you."

9. Ability to pass through the normal phases of relationship—from romance through conflict to commitment—with a love that matures within each vicissitude.

10. A commitment to an essential bond—an enduring "given" of mutuality—that weathers the stresses and crises of change. This bond is unconditional. If "someone else has come along" who is more attractive, more fun, "just right," it will be taken only as information about the charms of the new person or the deficits of the present relationship. It will not cause a break-up or lead to a new involvement.

The above ten elements describe unconditional love as it relates to intimate relationships.

II. Fears That Arise in Intimate Relationships

Primal fears arise in childhood that carry over into adult relationships:

- Fear of being abandoned and so losing the other; this makes us cling or be possessive of others.
- Fear of being engulfed and so losing oneself; this makes us run away or distance ourselves from others.

These are normal fears. Both arise in all of us—though one usually predominates in intimate relationships. It is only when these fears become so intense as to affect our judgment and behavior that they become problematic.

Adult relating is in the capacity to commit ourselves without being immobilized by the fear of abandonment if someone pulls too far away, or by the fear of engulfment if someone gets too close. It will seem as if these fears result directly from the behavior of our adult partner, but these are phantom fears. What is hurting us is gone but still stimulates. We are reacting to our own inner landscape, a landscape ravaged by archaic plunder that has never been acknowledged, restored, or forgiven. Heidegger says it in a striking way: "The Dreadful has already happened."

Since fears of abandonment and engulfment are thus cellular reflexes, we are wise not to take our partner's display of them too personally. These fears are not rational so we cannot talk someone out of them or blame someone for them. Compassion from one partner and work to change by the other partner is the most effective combination. (The "work to change" is described later in this section.)

Actually, an adult cannot be abandoned, only left, cannot be engulfed, only crowded! Once we live in the present, things become so much more matter-of-fact and we drop the blame-filled judgments.

Fear of Abandonment	**Fear of Engulfment**
Fear of independence so that one:	*Fear of dependency so that one:*
Has trouble letting go when the other needs space	Has trouble making a commitment
Seeks maximum contact (clings)	Seeks more space (distances)
Is enmeshed or obsessive about the other's story	Takes the other for granted or is indifferent
Is caretaking of the other and not of oneself	Feels entitled to need fulfillment by the other
Always wants to give more (sense of never giving enough)	Construes giving as obligating or receiving as smothering
Goes along with others' ideas, plans, or timing	Needs to be in control, to make decisions, or to be right
Has no personal boundaries or bottom line for abuse	Has no tolerance of disloyalty or inadequacy

Copes with any conduct	Has rigid boundaries with no tolerance of error
Is addicted to the other	Seduces the other and then withholds
Needs constant reassurance that the other will stay	Needs the other to "stay put while I come and go at will"
Fears aloneness	Becomes anxious with extended togetherness
Rationalizes (makes excuses that enable coping)	Intellectualizes (thinks or explains away feelings)
Protects the other from the impact of one's own feelings	Avoids or minimizes one's own and the other's feelings
Shows fear, represses anger	Shows anger, represses fear
Distress in comings/goings	Distress in giving/receiving
Manifests clinging, closeness, and reaching out	Manifests coldness, rigidity, and distance

III. Working with Abandonment and Engulfment Fears

Sometimes we choose relationships that stimulate one or both of these fears.

Sometimes we choose relationships that allay these fears. A conscious adult will explore personal motives and choices and honestly admit them.

When a fear is *stimulated*, we get an opportunity to work through it or we become more entrenched in it—usually blaming our partner.

When a fear is *allayed*, we can feel safe enough to risk more openness or we can become complacent—expecting our partner to protect and insulate us.

You know a relationship matters to you in a healthy way when you are willing to act over the awkwardness of the small but scary steps that lead to change:

1. Notice which behavior of yours leads to problems for you or your partner. See through such excuses as: "This is how I am!" or "But I'm right." Acknowledge the fear or pain behind any behavior or attitude that makes smooth relating difficult. *All you need to know is that the relationship is not working as it is.* Cut through reasons, blame, and self-justification and admit the need for change. Such admission has healing power because it ends denial and attends to the truth.

2. Once you have become conscious of the most frequent fears that have arisen in one or more relationships, tell prospective or new partners about them, e.g. "I want to be intimate but I have to admit I become uncomfortable with a lot of bodily contact, except in sex"—or—"I notice you spend a lot of time with your friends. I will probably feel threatened by that because I easily feel abandoned—even when you assure me of your commitment."

You may be reluctant to share your agenda for fear of losing your partner. Declare this fear openly, too! Then two things will probably follow:

a. Your self-esteem will increase because of your integrity in self-disclosure in spite of the fear of loss.

b. You will find out the nature of your partner's commitment.

3. Intimacy fears tend to surface after the romantic phase of a relationship. Abandonment and engulfment issues create a new kind of negative excitement: fear and thrill at the same time. The adrenalin rush can be addicting and can lead to your doing things that *stir up* the fears. Admit to this whether or not you see how you do it. Paradoxically, by taking responsibility for the unconscious choice element in your drama, you are freed from it.

4. If you fear abandonment, let your partner go one more inch away each day and notice that you survive it. Reassurances rein-

force the fear. Live through one more episode of fear—or one more day of an episode—without asking your partner for a reassurance that he or she will stay with you or still loves you. This reinforces your independence.

5. If you fear engulfment, let your partner get one inch closer every day and notice how you can stand it (or may even enjoy it). Remember that one inch represents 100% progress the first time you allow it!

You may feel the strong need to be in control and make all the decisions in the relationship. On small decisions, alternate with your partner so that you make one choice and the partner makes the next. On larger decisions, negotiate so that both of you get something each of you wants every time.

6. To fear engulfment is to believe that closeness takes something away from you. Deal with this fear of *losing* yourself paradoxically by *freely giving* yourself. Make a self-disclosure, admit a vulnerability, or show a feeling. Thus *you stop losing by letting go.*

To fear abandonment is to dread being left alone. This is a fear not of loss of self but of gain of self-confrontation. Setting time aside for yourself daily means *choosing* the very thing you fear. This paradoxical reversal leads gradually to your enjoying your aloneness.

Since the fear is maintained by a sense of ourselves as victims, choice releases its grip. Jung describes the healing power of paradox in this way: "If there is a fear of falling, the only safety consists in deliberately jumping."

IV. Practical Skills for Intimacy

- PROCESSING FEELINGS

The telling of an event over and over without feeling and closure is a form of avoidance since it does not lead to change. The story only helps us not to know our real feelings. Processing the feelings that arise from events leads to a sense of closure and getting on with our life. We depart from the story, struggle through the process, and reintegrate at a higher level of functioning.

Here is a format that may be helpful in processing the feelings that arise from situations and events that strongly affect one or both partners:

1. Identify the underlying feeling and name it to yourself. This may take talking it out with someone who is objective and perceptive and whom you can trust. Once you know the feeling you can explore its origin. Does it arise solely from the present context or does it trigger your own past distress from early life or from a pattern of old experiences?

Only after you have identified the feeling and understood its origin are you ready to express it effectively to your partner. Now you know what you really feel, how much is personal or historical and how much is interpersonal, and what to ask for. Check in with yourself and others continually about whether you are perceiving a reality or a picture you carry in your mind about how you wish something were. Mental pictures are subtle and seduce us constantly. It takes work to keep correcting ourselves back into reality.

2. Express the feeling to your partner verbally and non-verbally (gestures, voice and face changes, tears, etc.).

3. Ask your partner to acknowledge it, understand it, and care about it. Ask your partner to acknowledge his or her role in stimulating, or occasioning it. Your partner did not cause it since you are a responsible adult not a victim, but he or she is co-accountable for its having arisen.

At this point you can most accurately tell whether it is present or old business. If it is a truly present issue you will feel better for having expressed the feeling no matter what response you have received. You will take it all as information and ask for amends and change but not demand them. No matter what the outcome, you will easily let go. If it was a past issue of yours, you will get caught in drama, story-telling, being right, blaming, and demanding. Your own sense of closure will be thwarted because your reaction has put your partner on the defensive and communication cannot proceed easily. As a result, you cannot let go of what hurts even more! In such an instance, go back to your objective friend or therapist and work on releasing the past pain. An adult loves to find out where his work really lies, so he can lay it to rest once and for all.

The real meaning of "hard feelings" is old feelings that have become calcified and now hurt us whenever they are pricked. To process is to remove the archaic, painful deposits and liberate the soft, healthy vulnerability so close to our surface and so productive of loving responses in others.

• CONTAINING OUR FEELINGS

Feelings are meant to be expressed *and* contained. An adult shows feelings and does not use them as a pretext to be self-destructive or to hurt others. When someone hurts, angers, or leaves you, allow yourself to feel the pain and talk about it but do not act on the feelings. Express every feeling but act on none. You do not go looking for an assurance or a chance to be avenged or a way to manipulate or to alter the outcome. You contain your feelings and take responsibility for them as totally yours. Someone else has triggered the pain, but it is up to you to take care of yourself by:

1. Accepting the reality of another's action or decision, whether or not you see it as justified, and

2. Feeling the pain keenly without being so possessed by it that it devastates your self-esteem. Feeling but not acting on feelings is the way we let the experience in without letting it penetrate the core of our self-worth. "I acknowledge this reality even though I don't like it. It could be better or it could be worse."

3. Acknowledging that this painful event reminds you of similar ones from childhood. Old feelings about betrayal, abandonment, and rejection are restimulated by contemporary versions of them. The strong feelings we have now show us where our unmourned issues are. Acting on feelings in the present is thus anachronistic! Our present feelings reenact the past and so require no

present taking of action, only expression of the feelings as part of mourning for past pain.

Every relationship includes some hurt. You may hold on to your indignation or to the pursuit of vengeance after being offended by someone. This maintains your grievance and prevents you from ever getting on with mutual commitment. Resentments that are worked through and dropped are the pathfinders to commitment. Resentments that are avenged, held onto, or used as weapons ever after are the stumbling blocks preventing commitment.

To let go of the need for retribution releases you from the pain more powerfully than vengeance ever can. This is because now your life together has gone on in an unconditionally loving way. The hurts have become resolved facts, not stressful stabs at keeping old wounds open.

Every adult relationship requires conflict before true commitment can happen. Each struggle helps you discard yet another illusory ideal about the other person, yet another illusory title to have your expectations met. Every conflict clears away the sham in favor of a fuller revelation of this real person who has not met my every need or measured up to what I wanted, but my love for that person has survived. That is the unconditional love—grounded in reality and mutually liberating—by which true commitment flourishes.

The healthy adult acknowledges that feeling hurt is a universal human experience, always to be expected, never to be consciously inflicted. Such an adult seeks to handle hurt, not to hide from it. All the mythic and religious themes of life-through-death endorse the value and necessity of pain in the emergence of our full and authentic identity. Every hurt was what was somehow required so that we could get here, so that we could let this light through. "It takes just such evil and painful things for the great emancipation to occur," Nietzsche so powerfully reminds us.

Feeling hurt can be processed, worked through, and minimized as healthy relationships progress. When hurt is frequent and severe and cannot be worked through, it is abuse. This leads not to growth but to lower self-esteem and unredeeming suffering. Mature adults shun liaisons like this and move out of the line of fire to safer pastures.

• FEEDBACK

Cease protecting your partner from knowing how her behavior impacts on you. No adult (who is not hospitalized) is too fragile to receive honest feedback. No adult deserves to be blamed, but anyone can be called to account. Holding back your feelings can be a subtle way to avoid the confrontation that reveals to both of you how unacceptable things are. Your coping may be enabling self-defeating or abusive behavior to go on. Hoping may mean stalling for time. Coping and hoping work for you only when they accompany a solid ongoing program of change to which both of you are deeply committed.

• BEING RIGHT

Give your partner the gift of being right. This applies to emotions and to your partner's perceptions of you. It does not apply to finances, life/death, or abuse issues, nor to addictions or opinions that lead to dangerous consequences. Paradoxically, a person becomes more open to you when you acknowledge his intuitions as making sense. In the bargain, you let go of your own competitiveness, polarizing opposition, and adversarial distancing.

If the result of this process is that you feel wrong, then the point has been missed. We give the gift of being right because being right just does not matter. The need to be right is a form of holding on which is based on fear. Giving the gift of letting someone else be right compassionately allows both of you to relax. The fear eases away and the humor is released. Then the mutual trust level increases.

Once the accent is no longer on being right, you can truly hear the other person. You acknowledge her feeling and make amends for any way in which you may have been irresponsible. You can ask for this same acknowledgment and amendment when your partner seems irresponsible toward you. Who was right and who was wrong has now become irrelevant and the arrogance of the neurotic ego is succeeded by new humility.

• SENSE OF BEING OWED TO

The abiding sense that you are being cheated or that something is owed to you can lead you to take from others unfairly or to be ungenerous about giving. Waiting for a bargain or a discount price may be a signal that you believe something is owed to you. Work your way out of this by freely giving something to those you think owe you something and ceasing to take unfairly from them.

• SENSE OF OWING

The abiding sense that you owe something can lead you to be people-pleasing, overly generous, or always to "settle for less" in relationships. You may find that you cannot receive from others unless you owe them something. You may believe that you have to purchase others' affection, that it will never come unsought or unbought. (The price is always our own self-emergence.) Work with this by asking for a stringless gift—one that requires no gift in return—from those you think you are indebted to.

• COMPASSION

We may reckon an inability to give to be stinginess or constant giving with little ability to receive to be generosity. We may rightly consider an intrusive, controlling manner to be manipulative. We may perceive fear of speaking up or acceptance of abuse as cowardice or passivity. We may be impatient with someone who is afraid to be held or touched. We may think we are being rejected by someone who is afraid to show his feelings or someone who is so self-absorbed that he cannot focus on us.

As we allow our softer side to emerge, we notice a new dimension: every one of these negative qualities is actually a form of *pain*. No one wants to be afraid of closeness; it hurts to have that fear! A controlling person feels the pain of stress and of noticing that her mien alienates her from others' love! We deal assertively with the impact of all these behaviors on us: we report our feelings and misgivings; we ask for change. At the very same time, we feel compassion for the unattended pain behind every holding-back and holding-on. Our compassion does not stop us from taking care of ourselves, but it does make our sensitivity to pain acute. The more spiritually conscious we become, the more we allow ourselves to recognize the subtle face of pain and fear that lurks behind the behaviors we judge. "It is only with the heart that one sees rightly" (*The Little Prince*).

Spiritual compassion enlarges our generosity and integrity also. When we operate from a strong functional ego, our integrity makes us act fairly toward others. When we have integrated ego with spiritual wisdom, integrity engages a compassion that transcends fairness while always including it.

In a relationship, this may mean that both parties do not choose to use the same freedoms or limitations. For example: "You feel great pain when I form close outside relationships, even though they are not sexual. I feel no pain at all about your outside relating. To be fair, both of us have equal latitude in this area. To be compassionate, I give up the exercise of my right since it triggers so much hurt in you—without asking you for the same in return. Meanwhile, with compassion for me, you have committed yourself to working in therapy on your fear and jealousy so that eventually I can relate to others with no consequence to you."

The "double standard" refers to moral issues but not to consciously compassionate relationships.

• TIME OUT

In childhood we have full permission to cling, to go out of control, to have a temper tantrum or to be impractical. The wise parent allows this within limits. A healthy adulthood includes an occasional liberating visit to these familiar (but now scary) places. Our inner nurturant parent allows this flexibility within the limits of time, place, and responsibility.

One couple may, for instance, decide to go away for a weekend and to spend every minute together, clinging to each other for as long as they like. Another couple may choose a hiatus in their contact or separate vacation time. These circumstances could be planned or spontaneous but they are always timebound, conscious, and mutually negotiated. In this way we respect the routine of adulthood but take a safe break from it.

Each of us contains the opposite sides of every human possibility. To be fully sane, practical, centered, and fearless, we need to experience the other side occasionally. "Time out" provides for this creative compensation. The combination of self-permitting and timeboundedness is a humorous defiance of those "solid truths" about the folly of clinging. We honor the truths but slip by them for fun, like Ulysses, the trickster, who enjoyed the sirens' song while sailing safely by.

• DECIDING

In matters of the heart, thinking (ironically) leads only to more confusion. What works best is simply noticing:

—what your body feels;
—what your actions are;
—what your intuition keeps coming back to.

Noticing leads to knowing. You can trust this to happen automatically. Effort may only confound. The next best step appears when we pay attention to the parts of ourselves that cannot deceive: body, behavior, inner wisdom. A decision will feel right when it arrives unhurried and with a sense of belonging in all three of these personal territories.

The decision with wisdom usually finds a way not to exclude one side totally, not *either . . . or* but *both . . . and.* Such a decision embraces risk rather than avoids it. It is the decision with power but without control, with respect for others' wishes but with request for what one wants, with acknowledgment of one's history but with no enslavement to it.

Before making any serious or lasting decision, test yourself at wanting it consistently each day for one to six months: "I have to want to marry you for six months before I agree to set the date."

This same procedure can be used if you are ambivalent about returning to a former partner. Instead of denying your inclination or fighting it off, tell yourself you will seek reunion if you want it consistently every day for six months. Then you will feel no pressure or self-denial but a permission that honors the test of time and protects you from a precipitous decision.

• STALEMATE

Like a sailboat in a windless port, a relationship is sometimes unmoving and stuck. There is no joy, no problem, and no motivation for change. "If he would have an affair, I'd at least have a reason to leave!" But he instigates no facilitating crisis. I am faced with the totally adult predicament of having no one to blame and no one to precipitate an interruption of the mediocrity. We can both go on for years not going on with liveliness—"till death do us part."

How can the bind of Lord and Lady Deadlock be broken? The partner with the lower level of tolerance for boredom (i.e. the higher bottom line) takes the action. He does something—for his own pleasure—that is different, sudden, and surprising. This rivets attention on the mutual emptiness and activates radical alteration. It does not matter whether the change is "for better or for worse." Either result will blow you away from the sultry port.

• AT THE END

There are many levels of loss throughout distressed relationships. Each is a letdown; each bursts an illusion; each requires griefwork.

Here are examples of the checkpoints of loss in a relationship that has ended:

Certitude the relationship will work
Ends and leads to
↓
Hope it can work
Ends and takes action in
↓
Struggle to make it work
Ends and leads to
↓
Realization that it will not work

In a truly conscious relationship, each partner notices these endings and grieves the unique loss entailed in each of them. In most relationships, unfortunately, the shifts are imperceptible and unmourned. As a result, when the relationship ends, we are faced with all the unattended additive grief. The best signal of this is a sense of disappointment, bitter resentment, and self-pity that can recur for years.

Appropriate grief is current. It follows in the wake of each passing chance for success. True grief does not begin in divorce. It begins when the romance ends and then recommences with each hope that comes to naught.

The grief that is unnoticed, unprocessed, and never called by name actually contributes to the breakdown of relationships. A sense of defeat, anger, and blame gnaws at the bonds of love. Then a depression shadows us and we never quite know why.

Griefwork done mutually builds intimacy because it means sharing feelings, consciously and safely. When the sadness, anger, hurt, etc. of grief are experienced in the container of tender compassion, commitment grows. The very ability to allow ongoing grief and ongoing love to coexist may break the downward spiral of failure.

All the processes of grief outlined in Chapter 1 apply to the ending of a relationship. The worse the relationship, the longer is the mourning required. This is because we are letting go not only of the partner and the relationship but also of the illusory hope that it would work.

Sleep and appetite disorders are to be expected in a time of crisis. It is important to take care of oneself by eating and resting regularly but not excessively. It is also important to treat oneself to what one most enjoys without using drugs or alcohol to avoid the stress. This combination of self-nurturance and self-protection provides the best conditions for processing the loss that has occurred.

Stress prevents us from thinking clearly, so impulsive decisions—especially regarding finances, possessions, legal issues, or relocating—during this time are dangerous. Any thought is appropriate, but action requires long-term consideration and prior feedback from objective friends.

Separation leads to self-doubt. You may then believe you may never find another partner. This gives you information not about reality but about how wounded you feel. It is the fear element of grief and it recedes as your grief work proceeds. Gradually in the process of separation and grief you find out things about yourself (and your partner) that surprise and discourage you. You believe you are isolated and faced with a hopeless void. This is the same void most people avoid during relationships. It opens its jaws when denial ceases and we acknowledge our shadow side.

Grief work, with its cathartic experience of feelings, truly and finally bridges this abyss. We accept and forgive ourselves for not being perfect and we make amends where that is appropriate. Then the void becomes just the *spaciousness* we needed to greet ourselves authentically and to be renewed.

Obsessive or suicidal thoughts and repeating your story are perfectly normal and are to be allowed—as the nurturant parent allows the child to tell about her nightmare again and again. All that matters is that you do not act on the feelings or the thoughts by any attempts to hurt yourself or punish the other. Contain the feelings and thoughts within yourself and your own support system.

What works best is to allow every feeling and thought to pass through you as good hikers through the woods: taking nothing away, leaving nothing behind. Make no attempt to think them away, to interpret, or to interrupt them no matter how irrational or inconvenient they may seem. "The only way to live is like the rose: without a Why," as Meister Eckhart exclaims.

Be wary of contact with your former partner too soon after separation. The belief that you have something to tell her may mask a manipulation to change or punish her or to justify yourself. This distracts you from the fact of the ending and the grieving of it.

It is normal to feel love for, anger toward, and fear of a former partner, since the essential bond between you has been defeated, but not ended, by separation. This bond is unconditional and beyond the reach of betrayal, change, or divorce. In true grief work, we acknowledge this bond but no longer act upon it. *The bond remains but the transactions are ended.* Now we contain the love for—without having to take care of—the other. We contain the anger without having to gain satisfaction for it. We contain the fear without having to devise complex strategies to avoid chance meetings.

Grieving occurs best in the gap that opens in your life once you are alone. It cannot proceed while you are involved with some-one new. When a relationship has ended, the healthy adult allows adequate time alone for working through grief and for processing what has been learned. Time elapses and then readiness for a new relationship occurs. One neither seeks nor avoids but lets it come unsought. This is trusting the synchronous timing of the universe over inner urgency or social pressures.

One of the difficulties in moving out of the familiar is the temptation to close off the full drama of change before it ripens. *The sense of being bereft of all that is familiar is a vacuum which threatens to suck up everything within its reach.*

What is hard to appreciate, when terror shapes a catastrophic gap, is that this blankness can be a Fertile Void. The Fertile Void is the existential metaphor for giving up the familiar supports of the present and trusting the momentum of life to produce new opportunities and vistas.

The acrobat who swings from one trapeze to the next knows just when he must let go. He gauges his release exquisitely and for a moment he has nothing going for him but his own momentum. Our hearts follow his arc and we love him for risking the unsupported moment.

—Erving and Miriam Polster,
Gestalt Therapy Integrated

SUMMARY REFLECTIONS ON PART TWO: ADULT LIVING IN RELATIONSHIPS

The "Givens" of Relationships:
Antidotes to Unrealistic Expectations

All factors in relationships pass through phases: intimacy, affection, sexual interest/energy, commitment to children and family, compatibility, self-disclosure.

Only at rare moments is the love in one partner the same as that in the other.

Priorities are continually changing for each partner. The integrity of the union may not always be a priority.

No truly loving relationship takes away—or can take away—even one of your basic human rights.

Intimate relationships survive best with constant permission for ever-changing ratios of closeness and distance.

What *creates* distance in your relationship, you may be using unconsciously to *get* distance.

The best relationship includes space for you to pursue individual choices and to be compassionately attentive to any threat your partner may feel.

No one can control or change someone else, nor is it necessary.

No one is loyal or truthful all the time.

No expectations are valid and not even agreements are always reliable.

Your partner may not always be a consistent, nurturant, or a trust-worthy friend to you (nor you to your partner).

You are ultimately alone and ultimately able to make it alone.

No relationship can create self-esteem, only support it.

There is no one person who will make you happy, keep you fas-cinated, love you as your favorite parent did, or give you the love you missed from your parents.

Most people in relationships seldom know what they really want, ask for what they really want, or show what they really feel.

Most people avoid or fear intimacy, consistent honesty, intense feelings, and uninhibited joy.

Beneath every serious complaint about your partner is something unowned in yourself.

Letting go of blame and the need to be right heals a relationship most efficaciously.

Jealousy and possessiveness, though not desirable, are normal hu-man feelings.

"Goodbye" is rarely said clearly; most people ease away wordlessly and avoid full confrontation.

No one is to blame when a relationship ends.

The end of one relationship will always require a space before another relationship can begin healthily.

It is normal for memories, regrets, the wish for revenge, and a recurrent sense of loss far, far to outlast the ending of a relationship.

One of your (or your partner's) parents is a phantom, but active, presence at the beginning, middle, or ending of your relation-ship.

The powerful appeal of someone new may tell you more about your own neediness than about the charms of the other person.

A relationship is a spiritual path since it consists of a continual shedding of illusions.

> *Throughout all eternity,*
> *I forgive you,*
> *You forgive me.*
> —William Blake
> to his wife

part three

Integration

9. THE ART OF
FLEXIBLE INTEGRATION

*Somewhere in the heart of experience, there is an order and
a coherence which we might surprise if we were attentive
enough, loving enough, or patient enough. Will there be time?*
        —Lawrence Durrell: *Justine*

The process of personal integration is one of containment,
not of elimination. We have integrated a healthy ego when we
comfortably contain the full spectrum of our thoughts and behavior, both the positive and the negative, i.e. "I am much more assertive now but occasionally still passive." We are hard on ourselves
when we demand total elimination of all our shortcomings.

Integration is a human not a mechanical process. It has a
unique timing over which we have no control. Integration does not
mean that a problem has been totally solved and will never recur,
e.g. "My becoming more aware of your feelings does not ensure
that I will be there for you every time."

To integrate is to contain comfortably both ends of the spectrum of change. For example, we will become authentic in our
self-presentation and at the same time we will still occasionally dis-
semble. Integration is not total anything; it is simply a rearranging of
the proportions of life. Now we are more open and less guarded
but both styles still appear in our overall behavior.

While in a monogamous relationship, I have sexual desire for
someone else. Integration does not mean violating my experience
by rooting out the desire. I contain the desire, but instead of acting
on it, I look into what it may be saying to me (and us). In this way, I
am faithful to my inner life *and* to my relationships.

Once we acknowledge that true change does not have to
mean becoming totally different we become lighter and happier.

We are satisfied simply with increasing positives and decreasing negatives. We are more respectful of the graceful and inscrutable seasons of human transformation, always one part effort and one part timing. We acknowledge and ask others to acknowledge this in us and in themselves. "The wisdom of equanimity, imbued with generosity, sees all situations equally as ornaments of being," as the Tibetan Buddhist teacher, Trungpa Rinpoche, observes.

> I am my present and my past so new insights will coexist with antiquated beliefs. Instead of attempting to rid myself of my old beliefs, I simply no longer act on them. I allow the atavistic beliefs to be present and I act more and more in accord with the new, better informed, convictions. I contain new behaviors simultaneously with old beliefs and habits:
> 1. I accept challenges while still feeling afraid.
> 2. I trust someone while still doubting.
> 3. I choose pleasures that may have an element of risk.
> 4. I let go of punitiveness while still feeling vengeful.
> 5. I ask for what I want generally while still allowing this strong desire to remain a wish.
> 6. My self-esteem coexists with occasional self-reproach.
> 7. I feel anxious without taking it out on anyone.

If the ratio always remains the same or keeps altering in favor of what is negative and self-defeating, we are not evolving. If the ratio is changing in favor of the positive—even a moment or inch at a time—we are growing.

We know we are not integrating the full spectrum of our feelings when we keep reducing them all to a single judgment. For example, "I am emotionally stuck," may also mean: "I am depressed and grieving and self-pitying and refusing to self-activate." Or "I am a loving father" may need to be expanded to "I am a loving father in many ways and there are also times when I am controlling and put my own expectations ahead of my children's needs."

Noticing when we disregard the full spectrum of our feelings and behavior and then acknowledging our missing predicates may enrich our sense of our own depth! "From now on, every time I judge myself (or others), I will use the technique of adding four more adjectives that are also somehow true!"

Acknowledge openly to others that sometimes you succeed and sometimes you fail; sometimes you come through for them and sometimes you let them down. You offer to come through for someone just one more time than you let someone down. You offer not perfection but commitment to make amends for failures, to make restitution for losses. This is a *flexible* (and therefore adult) presentation of your self. It preserves you from the expectation by others that you can be counted on absolutely, or the verdict of others that you be discounted absolutely. "To live is to change and to be perfect is to have changed often," as Cardinal Newman so wisely remarked. It would be a great violation of humanness to be rigidly perfect in conduct. The repressive vigilance such white-knuckling requires does not signify an achievement but a self-defacement.

If our self-actualization means that our inner work must all be done and we must be perfect, we are choosing never to be happy. No human being is perfect like that, except momentarily. If integration means wholly containing a process, then, as St. Catherine of Siena says, "All the way to heaven is heaven." We are complete now and all along the path.

The hero's journey metaphor powerfully illustrates this. Every step on the path is sacred: the original crossing of the threshhold, the struggle, the return with higher consciousness. The hero is always complete because he is acting in accord with here and now unfolding challenges. The struggle is thus equal in value to the prize because both honor what that moment can offer. Full self-esteem thus is ours while we confront our fears, work on them, and integrate them. Then "wholeness is completeness, not perfection," as Jung noted.

Chemical elements cannot be transformed into something new while they remain carefully separated and distinct. When they are mixed together—contained—in a vessel, they become something more than both originally were. The psyche is that vessel accommodating disparate thoughts and feelings that coexist in us, no matter how unlikely they seem for union. How fitting that the "sacred marriage of opposites" is such an ancient and universal symbol of spiritual fulfillment!

> I try to help people . . . experience their spiritual connectedness by helping them get in touch with both their tenderness and their power. I don't think there's such a thing as instant intimacy or instant spirituality—these are things that evolve in us. To reach them . . . we need to see that . . . we are born to evolve. . . . It is a growing thing—and there is no fear in it. Not that we haven't heard the message before. It's what Christ talked about, and the Buddha, and others. But in the past most of us . . . said, "They're beyond us, they're divine . . . we're nothing but humans, so we can't make the same connection." But now, we're beginning to know that we can.
>
> —Virginia Satir

10. BEFRIENDING THE SHADOW

We meet ourselves in a thousand disguises along the path.
—Jung

The Shadow is the archetype of the unconscious that represents the feared, denied, unaddressed, forbidden, and excluded parts of ourselves. Joseph Campbell calls the Shadow "the inconvenient or resisted psychic powers that we have not dared to integrate." We project these powers (characteristics) onto others of our same sex and react strongly to them.

The negative Shadow is composed of our own unacceptable and disowned defects that we strongly condemn in others. What we are unconscious of in ourselves, we become emphatically conscious of in others.

The positive Shadow is composed of the good qualities hidden in us that we strongly admire or envy in others. We consciously respect in them what we inwardly disavow in ourselves. "In every work of genius, we can recognize our own rejected thoughts. They come back to us with a certain alienated majesty" (Emerson).

I and It

The Shadow turns some of our "I" (what is really ourselves) into "It" (which seems to exist only in others). Befriending the Shadow means restoring our "I" to its wholeness by taking back—recollecting—all our projected, banished parts. "Where It was, there I shall be" (Freud).

What we exclude and disown becomes larger than life. It turns on us and scares us. We are then hurt by an unlived part of our very selves. To recollect or integrate our projections is to acknowledge them and let them back in. Then we contain all the parts of ourselves. This is the meaning of psychological healing: acknowledging what we have denied and restoring the full complement of our own powers.

We drop defenses long enough to admit and allow that the negative "out there" is somehow "in here." Then we automatically discover its inner core of positive value and personal enrichment. To drop defenses is to depart from the neurotic attachment of ego. It is to reach a coherently healthy ego.

Beauty accepted the Beast while he was still ugly and so found the Prince, beautiful like her, i.e. her partner, her missing part, her other half. She enlisted the very energy that she had once feared and disenfranchised. Her foe then became her ally, no longer larger than life but life-size. She discovered an identity with him. This is the spiritual self, the same in all of us, released by unconditional love.

Integrating the Positive Shadow

To integrate the positive Shadow is to acknowledge our own untapped potential behind the awe we have of others. We begin to acknowledge and to release from within ourselves the very talents and qualities we admired in others. At first this means "acting as if" but soon we act with ease and even more of our hidden powers become accessible to us. We expend effort and then grace takes over.

Integrating the Negative Shadow

To integrate the negative Shadow, we admit—without at first seeing the justification—that we have the very characteristic we so disparage in someone else. We drop blame and discover a valuable kernel. We then find in ourselves this positive, but still unlived, counterpart of the negative quality we see in another. Hidden in everything negative is something alive and beautiful that wants to belong to us (as the Prince within the Beast wanted to belong to Beauty). *Negative only means not yet redeemed by conscious integration.*

What follows is a list of the counterparts of the negative Shadow. As you acknowledge anything you strongly dislike in others (left column), you are challenged to adopt its equivalent positive lively quality for yourself (right column).

PROJECTED *If you are strongly upset by others':*	UNOWNED *Then you have but may not be using your own:*
Addictiveness	Steadfastness
Anxiety	Excitement
Approval seeking	Openness to appreciation
Arrogance	Self-confidence
Bias	Discernment
Bitterness, grudge-holding	Refusal to overlook injustice
Caretaking	Compassion
Clinging	Loyalty
Compromise	Negotiability
Compulsive orderliness	Organization, efficiency
Conning	Teaching, encouraging
Connivance	Intelligent strategizing
Control, manipulativeness	Leadership, efficiency, coordinating ability
Cowardice	Caution
Cruelty	Anger
Cunning	Forethought
Defensiveness	Preparedness
Demanding	Asking
Dependency on others	Reasonable trust of others
Flattery	Complimenting

PROJECTED *If you are strongly upset by others':*	UNOWNED *Then you have but may not be using your own:*
Foolhardiness	Bravery
Greed	Self-provision
Guilt	Conscientiousness
Hostility	Assertiveness
Hypocrisy	Ability to "Act as if"
Impatience	Eagerness
Impulsiveness	Spontaneity
Incompetence	Willingness to experiment
Indecision	Openness to possibilities
Insensitivity	Objectivity
Intimidation	Confrontation
Jealousy	Protectiveness
Jumping to conclusions	Intuitiveness
Lack of order	Flexibility
Laziness	Relaxedness
Loneliness	Openness to nurturance
Loquacity	Articulateness
Lying	Imaginativeness
Neediness	Asks for respect of appropriate needs
Obsequiousness	Respect
Perfectionism	Commitment to do things well
Procrastination	Honoring one's own timing
Rigidity	Tenacity
Sarcasm	Wit
Selfishness	Self-nurturance
Self-pity	Self-forgiveness

PROJECTED *If you are strongly upset by others':*	**UNOWNED** *Then you have but may not be using your own:*
Sense of obligation	Choice
Slyness	Shrewdness
Submissiveness	Cooperation, docility
Tactless bluntness	Frank candidness
Taking for granted	Accepting
Vengefulness	Justice

Using the preceding listings, here is a way of working with the negative shadow:

I am strongly upset when others are **controlling.**

I acknowledge that I am **controlling,** though I may not see it right now.

I have **efficiency** and **leadership skills** that I have not fully used.

I choose to *act as if* I had a high level of **leadership ability** without being **controlling.**

An automatic shift will then occur with three results:

1. Controlling behavior by others will become simply an object of observation. You will be informed, but not affected by it. You will be a witness, not an antagonist.

2. Your own subtly controlling ways will vanish.

3. Your coordinating and leadership skills will emerge automatically and with ease.

Only that which is really ourselves has the power to heal.
—Jung

11. DREAMS AND DESTINY: SEEING IN THE DARK

Dreams prepare, announce or warn about situations long before they happen. This is not a miracle or precognition. Most crises have a long incubation in the unconscious.

—Jung

Dreams are messages from the unconscious that show us where we are on our path, where our struggle lies, and where our destiny awaits us. Our destiny is to let the light of consciousness penetrate the dark unlived corners of our selves and our world. Dreams take us to those corners. Dreams tell us what we do not know yet, never what we already know. Like the Shadow, they show us the face we hide, the disavowed or neglected sides of ourselves. What we have excluded in conscious life comes to us in dreams and asks to be included, that is, consolidated in wholeness. In this sense, dreams reconcile conscious and unconscious, another way of describing our destiny.

Dreams are agents of change. When we listen to dreams, they lead us into our deeper, interior, undiscovered world. "Deeper" means that a stronger and more enriching bond has been forged between our conscious and unconscious life.

Practical Information

Everyone dreams every night, usually at ninety minute intervals. Dreams in the early part of the night last one to two minutes, in the latter part up to an hour. Dreams are stored in the short term memory and so are easily forgotten, no matter how clearly we may remember them when we first awaken. We all dream in color but the color is forgotten first.

Dreams use the events of the preceding day as props to tell their story. It is important, therefore, not to explain away or minimize the significance of a dream by saying, "I dreamed that only because yesterday I . . ."

Anyone can remember dreams:

1. Drop the negation "I don't remember dreams."

2. Affirm throughout the day and while falling asleep: "I remember my dreams."

3. Use auto-suggestion while lying in bed waiting to fall asleep, "I will wake up in time to write down my dreams and will easily fall back to sleep."

4. Keep paper, pen, and light near your bed and write immediately upon waking whatever you remember, no matter how fragmentary. If you remember nothing at first, write anything that enters your mind at that moment. Practice will lead to results. Do not write in paragraphs, only in phrases that tell the gist of the dream. Include feelings upon waking, mood and colors in the dream, the setting, exposition, and conclusion of the dream.

5. Keep a dream journal into which you transcribe daily the full text of your dreams.

6. Tell your dreams to someone else.

7. Use the Active Imagination techniques daily (described below).

By respecting dreams in each of these seven ways you are more likely to remember them and receive their message. Jung says: "Attention to the unconscious pays it a compliment that guarantees its cooperation."

Recurrent Dreams

Most people have dreams that recur throughout life or for periods of life. Such dreams may have the following purposes:

1. To compensate for a deficiency in conscious life.

2. To anticipate a change, transition, or spiritual transformation.

3. To assimilate a physical or psychological trauma (since shock is best absorbed by repetition).

4. To demonstrate normal anxiety about unpreparedness, lateness, loss of control, world disaster, immobility, or rescue fantasies.

In working with recurrent dreams, simply notice how their details may change and point to more or less integration of the issue they present. Secondly, let the recurrent themes show you where your anxieties, griefs, or deficiencies lie so you can pay more attention to them.

Recurrent dreams are not so much to be interpreted as to be exhausted. They are played repeatedly like dramas, until integration and closure happen naturally.

Nightmares

A nightmare is a dream from which we awaken in terror. It is shock therapy from within. It is the way the unconscious italicizes its message, making it so striking or startling that it compels attention. It is important to let a nightmare continue past the point of fear, confronting the fearsome characters and asking their purpose. This may not be possible within the dream but it can be done by reimagining it upon awakening.

Remember that horrible nightmares and crude or sadistic images in dreams do not mean you are a bad person with terrible things inside you. Everyone of us has every possible human image stored within us, as neutrally as a dictionary does.

There are no bad dreams. Every dream gives us needed information about what we have not yet brought to the light, not yet transformed. Fear in a dream reveals the Shadow who asks for befriending. Change the statement "This is how bad I am" to "This is how badly I need to know this, or to do this, or to include this."

Incubation

Incubation of dreams is an ancient practice that gained prominence in the temples of Asclepius, god of healing. To incubate a dream is to evoke a dream in response to an immediate concern. In effect, you are consulting your own wholeness that mediates wisdom and healing through dreams.

Here is a threefold technique that may facilitate the process. First, focus on the concern or question throughout the day and as you fall asleep. Second, ask your inner mind for an answer, and, third, promise a gift of thanks if you receive one. The gift can be a favor to someone, a volunteering of time, a donation, etc.

Active Imagination

Dreams come from an interior knowledge that is larger than ego but requires the cooperation of ego to be understood. Our unlettered human nature speaks in approximations, symbols, and metaphors to reconnect us to the split off parts of ourselves. Every character and object in a dream is symbolic of a part of ourselves that asks for attention. Symbols are highly personal and individualized, so books defining them have little value.

Active Imagination is a Jungian technique for engaging with symbols of the unconscious and locating their unique meanings. It is cooperative work between conscious and unconscious whereby we dialogue with dream figures to discover and activate their message. Actually, every powerful and compelling image (especially one that has endured throughout the years) can be engaged by using this same technique.

Consciously to explore an image that has arisen from the unconscious is to experience the deepest part of oneself. Active Imagination is to the Self what therapeutic processing is to the ego. Images are to the Self what thoughts are to the mind.

In Active Imagination, symbols reveal and activate hidden truths about ourselves. Anything that can be visualized and then engaged imaginatively thereby becomes a vehicle of self-disclosure and spiritual transformation.

Jung speaks to this when he notes that "myths and symbols express the processes of the psyche far more trenchantly and clearly than the clearest concept, for the symbol conveys not only a visualization . . . but also a re-experiencing. It is a twilight we can only understand by inoffensive empathy which too much clarity dispels."

An Active Imagination format:
   I. Use meditation to empty your mind of thoughts. (See the next chapter for an example of a meditation technique.)
   II. Affirm an attitude of listening to your unconscious, not dictating to it.
   "I open myself to inner messages."
   "I am ready to know what I need to know."
   "I acknowledge my imagination as a faculty of healing."
   III. Dialogue with the image in writing, drawing, or movement without interpreting it.
   This dialogue develops from a felt sense of:
   • the image as I receive it, not as I prefer it,
   • what it says with no prompting from me,
   • my response without recourse to logic or discursive thought,
   • my spontaneous intuitions.
   IV. Create an affirmation that declares any result that has come from this process, e.g. "I forgive more and more."
   V. A ritual or action that enacts the result and honors the gift received.

Here is a way of working with an image that may be helpful in establishing the dialogue in Part III.
   1. Draw a circle with a picture or word for the image in it and with eight lines as tangents to it. Write an association with the image on each line. Do not use synonyms, definitions,

or simple descriptions. Do not base one word on the preceding word, as in free association. Return on each of the eight lines to the original image and let a word or phrase arise spontaneously.

2. Choose the most striking or surprising phrase of the eight that has been evoked.
3. Turn it into a question to you or a request of you.
4. Respond without thinking.
5. Evoke the power of the original image to translate this response into a practical plan.

Image and Contemplation

The Active Imagination technique outlined above is helpful in dreamwork. At the same time, the images presented in dreams have a transcendent power that defies technique. Simply staying with an image without any plan to shape a message out of it is a form of contemplation. Such empathy with the image may lead to a subtle inner shift that makes dreamwork more richly spiritual.

Jung *identified* image with psyche. In a transpersonal context, a dream image does not stand for something else. It is irreducible, and refers to itself. It is independent of mental constructs, neither pointing to another reality nor determined by one. A dream image is not a product of the imagination; it is a mirror of the self. It is not a symbol but an actuality. This is why contemplative wonder in the face of an image is so profoundly rewarding.

It is not necessary to elaborate meanings from an image. An image elaborates itself when we simply sit with it—as Christ revealed his wholeness at Emmaus when the disciples simply sat with him. Meanings we impose on or seek from images only silence them. An image is meant to be witnessed, not grasped, to be protected, not consumed, and to be honored, not used. Trust the image that has come to you in a dream and make room for it as a real presence in your life. It is the real presence of you.

There is an inner wholeness that presses its still unfulfilled claims upon us.

—Emma Jung

12. EGO/SELF AXIS: WHERE PSYCHOLOGY AND SPIRITUALITY MEET

In the hour of reconciliation, great marvels appear.
—Jung

The Synergy of Ego and Self

Psychological and spiritual work—both necessary for full human realization—are meant to proceed both separately and simultaneously as life unfolds. Effective psychotherapy attends to both ego and Self and is the primary form of help in the process of change and transformation.

Psychological work is a linear chronology leading us from problem to solution, from inadequacy to competence, from dysfunction to high level functioning.

Spiritual work is a journey from the compelling attachments of the neurotic ego to a Here-and-Now centered Self. This journey has no goal, as in the ego's effort-oriented work. It is a path that takes us back home to ourselves where a sacred marriage of all that heretofore seemed irreconcilable awaits us. Everything in life then fits. It is all just what we needed to achieve our destiny of conscious wholeness. "My destiny is to create more consciousness. The sole purpose of human existence is to kindle a light in the darkness of mere being," Jung wrote toward the end of his life.

The ego's ultimate work is to create enough sane ground so that the Self can grow its single imperishable Rose that lives by light. Both ego work and spiritual work combine effort (gain through pain) and effortless shifts (gain through grace). We move ourselves and we are moved onward as a rider spurs a horse and is then moved in the direction the horse is going. The steps we take in ego work shift us gently and automatically into insight and into healthier ways of being and relating. Spiritual work shifts us into enlightenment, i.e. letting the light through! "Enlightenment is the light that wholeness brings," says Von Franz.

In both these strands of our human tapestry—as in evolution—there are occasional unplanned and unplannable spurts of quantum growth. We are then receiving the grace (gift) of progress beyond our own effort or control. We begin noticing new sources of power or of oracular wisdom both within and around us. Our only response to such a miracle is giving thanks: our most efficacious form of communication with the visible–invisible Self.

An example of the congruence of psychological and spiritual work is in dealing with the hurts of childhood. Psychologically, we work *through* the emotions by grieving the past and by self-parenting. Spiritually, we work *with* the past experiences as present healing images. These images may reveal that what wounded us also sensitized us. We needed all the experiences of our life— positive and negative—to become as emotionally and spiritually rich as we are! "My barn having burned down, I now can see the moon," the Zen saying goes.

As we learn to honor timing, we may notice that we alternate between psychological and spiritual emphases in life. At one time, our main motive may be to seek out and respond to challenges, to take hold and become deeply involved in projects and relationships. This is functional ego work and takes rightful precedence over letting go. At another time, what will work best for us are choices that lead to fewer encumbrances, to lightening up, and letting go. This is spiritual unfolding and takes precedence over ego goals.

Psychological work ultimately leads us to closure and to the goal of change: healthier self-esteem and more productive relationships. Spiritual work leads us to continual transformations of consciousness: an ever-actualizing Self, in touch with inner healing powers both for us and for others. In this transformed state, we feel a sense of the numinous, gracious to us, a blissful and loving oceanic oneness with all beings and things, a reconciliation of apparent opposites and a realization that, though all of this is known in one simultaneous instant, no word can ever describe it.

Axis for Individuation

Our individuation, i.e. mature self-realization, as human beings can never occur within a disembodied spirituality that forsakes the ego or the body. Nor can it occur while the neurotic ego—with its fear of spiritual heights—maintains its inflated illusion that there is nothing beyond itself. It is only in an easy axis of ego and Self that we can access all our powers and display in time what is timelessly within us. "This perishable nature is meant for imperishability; this mortal frame is meant for immortality" (1 Cor 15:53).

In such a balance, the ego never again holds up or holds on to any transitory reality as permanently reliable. "Abide, thou art so fair!" (*Faust*). Rather, it enjoys a continual play of grasping and letting go, giving and receiving, working on what yields to change and resting with what does not yield.

Then the Self is hearkened to as it says the only word it knows: Yes—unconditionally and lovingly—to "what is past or passing or to come" and yet is always only Now. "In the end, the only events in life worth telling are those in which the imperishable world erupted into this transitory world," Jung wrote at the end of his life. Our journey, after all, was from and through the transitory to the imperishable, i.e. from ego attachments through ego strength to the unconditional love that is our spiritual self.

Meditation

Meditation provides a break from concentration on goals. In meditation we get in touch with that place in ourselves where we are perfect *without having to do anything*. The opposite of this is being attached to planning, analyzing, controlling, and trying to make things come out our way. Instead, we can simply accept our present situation and honor it as perfect. This opens us and change happens naturally.

We do not meditate to become serene, but only to be here now. Serenity and centeredness happen as we let go of everything that prevents us from being here now—e.g. thoughts, wishes, expectations, attachments.

Sitting meditation is usually done cross-legged or on a chair with back straight, head erect, hands on thighs or knees, breathing naturally and evenly, with mouth closed and eyes open. Keeping your eyes open fosters being here now rather than shutting out present reality. Do not stare at the floor; simply see it without concentrating on it. In fact, do not concentrate on anything; only maintain awareness of your breathing.

Do not try to get rid of thoughts or treat them as distractions. Let your thoughts pass *through* your mind without holding on to any one of them. Simply observe them without judgment or attachment, as if they were part of a movie.

This is actually a way of practicing for life: you do not have to be caught up in the drama in your head. You can be the watcher within who sees with full awareness but without anxiety or self-reproach. You can let what occurs inform you rather than overwhelm you.

When you notice yourself drifting with your thoughts, label it "thinking" and return to awareness of your breathing. In this way you remind yourself that you can choose to leave your personal storyline and come back to the here and now.

Meditation thus empowers you to acknowledge your present predicament as a light on the next step of your path and so to get on with your life. This is how the present is perfect.

Steps in Psychological Work Leading to Change

1. Letting go of neurotic ego attachments, control, and entitlement

NOT: "This has to come out my way."
BUT: "I let go of having to have this come out my way."
2. Unconditional Yes to what is occurring in events, feelings, circumstances:
"I allow this fully. I trust it without having to know why."

Shifts in Spiritual Self Leading to Transformation

1. Something new appears and with it the
2. Power to act in accord with the exigencies that face me.
3. Now I have the intuitive vision to see:
Where I held on and thereby was held back.
Where I can let go and thereby go on.
Where I said No and thereby interrupted my journey.
Where I can say Yes and thereby advance my journey.

We spend our lives waiting for the great day, the great battle, or the great deed of power. But that external consummation is not given to many, nor is it necessary. So long as our being is tensed passionately into the spirit in everything, then that spirit will emerge from our hidden, nameless efforts.

To reach these priceless layers is to experience with equal truth that one has need of everything and that one has need of nothing. Everything is needed because the world will never be large enough to quench our tastes . . . and yet nothing is needed because the only reality that can satisfy us lies beyond the transparencies in which it is mirrored. But everything that fades away and dies between us and it will only give reality back to us with greater purity after all. Everything means both everything and nothing. Everything is God to me and everything is dust.

—Teilhard de Chardin

13. UNCONDITIONAL LOVE

Stony limits cannot hold love out,
And what love can do, that dares love attempt.
—Romeo and Juliet

Love is our finest human grace.

It is unconditioned by expectation, neediness, or the desire to change, control, or rescue anyone.

Love lets go and never clings or controls.

It takes nothing away from us; it multiplies when we share it.

Whatever is true about love is true about each of us.

Love and we are just one miracle.

Our very identity is unconditional love. It is not something to be achieved. It is what we always were and already are. It is experienced uniquely and differently by each of us.

Every choice in life supports or denies this one penetrating fact.

Every risk is a challenge to love more.

Everything that happens in and through us is about this love: how we can see it, how we can show it.

In a very real way, we are who we are because of the love others have shown us. Our every adult asset began as a gift from someone who loved us as we were and thereby encouraged our unique self-emergence.

Our origin was in this living dialogue of love. We are still alive because of love.

Love is not an emotion but an unsentimental Being-Here-Now: generously, non-hurtfully, powerfully, truthfully, consciously.

Once love means consciously choosing to Be-Here-Now in an unconditional way, we can love not only people but the "What Is" of our life.

Love gives us the courage to see what is, to see it all as wise, to see it all as the very best predicament in which we can become free. Jung recommends "an affirmation of things as they are, an unconditional Yes to that which is . . . an acceptance of the conditions of existence."

Each person, thing, or event wants us to love it and when we do, it tells us its once-silent secret: everything is an imperishable Yes.

The starting point of our love for others is our sane and fearless love of ourselves.

When we look in the mirror and see a scared face, we are only seeing habit and conditioning. Our real image is of power and love, waiting to be acknowledged.

We love ourselves by showing our feelings, by being tender toward the places in ourselves that we do not like or that scare us, and by not staying in addictive or abusive relationships or circumstances. We move on to horizons that offer nurturance and that honor our deep lovability.

In these ways we embrace our destiny to demonstrate in time the timeless love we are—"else a great prince in prison lies."

Love is all that can satisfy the mute irrepressible longing we carry inside us. Our life will always feel strangely deficient until unconditional love happens. Only then do we realize what had been missing all along. Only then do deserts bloom.

The most perplexing and elusive mystery about love is that we can show it totally and yet we can never really know how much we love someone or just how intensely we are loved.

It is deeper than we can imagine or ever have imagined.

Sometimes a wink, a touch, a word, or a gift reveals a depth of love we never guessed was there. But not even then do we know the full extent of the love, only of its striking, sustaining, and momentary manifestations.

The limitation is in our minds which do not have the capacity to conceive or appreciate how profound love is. Our actions can show it all but our minds cannot let it all in.

Love is ineffable. We can never adequately put our love into words because words are categories of our minds and love is a living experience.

This is why love is such a unique mystery: We actually contain and channel a power that is greater than ourselves.

How poignant and bewildering that we have intellects inadequate to grasp the most precious of all realities! "Such are the tears of things."

The more we advance on our spiritual path, the more we appreciate that everything good, everything beautiful, everything life-affirming—even pain—is actaully love.

We can enjoy the beauty of Mozart's music. Then one day we realize that the beauty is only a felicitous trick he uses to bear us away to a realm where we feel loved. The cadences stroke us affectionately. They release the infinite within the limits of finitude.

We discover the gift dimension of the music and feel it in our bodies. We find out why it has survived the ages: it shows love and helps us receive it. "We are put on earth a little space, that we may learn to bear the beams of love," says William Blake.

Then we know that music is what love sounds like, and art, drama, and dance are what love looks like. When something still has the power to move us, it must have been love all along, since love moves the earth and other stars.

Unconditional love is what we have looked for whenever and wherever we looked for anything in relationships, in sex, in people-pleasing, in family ties, in any ties.

All the while it has been here within us and here everywhere around us. The only search is for that which is always and already ours.

What makes us human beings so uniquely wonderful in this puzzling universe is that we never give up on love.

Against all odds, with no guarantee of being loved in return, out of the hate and hurt so often handed us, in the face of the meaningless suffering history has let us see, we go on loving. We make a door of every gaping hole.

What deep respect we deserve for this capacity of ours to take what fate chooses for us and to make a choice of love in return!

How can we ever doubt the specialness of the part we play on this planet? What honor we deserve for handling, consciously and indefatigably, the most delicate and tender task of evolution: to make love out of nothing and to let it last.

Our experience is that human beings live on. From this I infer that it is the law of love that rules mankind. It gives me ineffable joy to go on trying to prove that.

—Gandhi

SUMMARY REFLECTIONS ON PART THREE: AFFIRMATIONS

For all that has been: Thanks!
For all that will be: Yes!
—Dag Hammarskjöld

Repeat any of these statements often throughout the day to release the receptive, softer side of yourself.

I accept this reality: This is my Body.

I surrender to every This and Now.

My love lets in what fear shuts out.

I parent myself.

More and more I yield and make peace.

I drop "shoulds"; I make choices.

I always have a choice.

I walk freely on the earth.

I have power: I let go of the need to control.

I drop guilt: I deserve pleasure and power.

I drop effort and all that I need comes to me.

I do what I need to do and trust the universe to carry me through.

I have what I need and need what I get.

Whatever happens to me is for me.

Whatever happens to me helps me grow up.

I love others more as I let go of any sense of obligation toward them.

Wonderful changes are happening in me; I allow them.

My sexual choices make me feel better and better about myself.

I am always and already what I most want to be.

I am over the fear that I never have enough.

My life is rich and complete; I am rich and complete.

I have enough; I have abundance.

I lighten up on myself and others.

I show my love.

I notice, receive and appreciate the authentic love others show me.

I bring out love in others.

I am loved and appreciated by everyone who is important to me.

I acknowledge as my own potential what I strongly admire in others.

I acknowledge what I despise in others as a denied part of myself.

I transform every defect into a capacity.

I am important to this planet.

I am thankful to be so rich in love.

Every beat of my heart releases love into the world.

I choose reconciliation and forgiveness; I let go of the need for revenge.

I feel abundant love within me and release it.

I grant myself abundance, again and again.

Everyone and everything is my teacher.

I allow my feelings and they become a Path.

The universe supports me as a joyful person.

The universe supports my every transition.

I am perfect Here-and-Now and honor myself as I am.

I have all the light and skill I need to take this next step.

I mend my conflict with circumstances.

I honor my present predicament as perfect.

I find wisdom and power in this predicament.

I honor others' choices.

I shed compassion on my world.

I am gentle toward my inner fears.

I risk unsupported moments.

I open myself to support.

I let go and go on.

I allow myself to be happy.

I ask for what I want and let the chips fall where they may.

I ask for what I want from others and let go of my insistence that they provide it.

I allow others to say No to me and take it as information.

I drop distancing and thereby learn how much space I need.

I love myself just as I am, day by day.

I have more and more to give away and give it.

I receive more and more.

I illuminate my world with love.

I accept everything in my past as complete and perfect.

Now I see it all with love and amusement.

> *Moment by moment,*
> *things are losing their hardness;*
> *now even my body lets the light through.*
> —Virginia Woolf

I'm ceded, I've stopped being Theirs—
The name They dropped upon my face
With water, in the country church
Is finished using now,
And They can put it with my Dolls,
My childhood, and the string of spools,
I've finished threading—too—

Baptized, before, without the choice,
But this time, consciously, of Grace—
Unto supremest name—
Called to my Full—The Crescent dropped—
Existence's whole Arc, filled up
With one small Diadem.

My second rank—too small the first—
Crowned—Crowing—on my Father's breast—
A half-unconscious Queen—
But this time—Adequate—Erect,
With Will to choose, or to reject,
And I choose: just a Crown—
                              —Emily Dickinson

From: *Complete Poems of Emily Dickinson*. Boston: Little, Brown, & Co., 1960.

SUGGESTED READING

Bolen, Jean S. *Goddesses in Every Woman*. New York: Harper and Row, 1984.

————. *The Tao of Psychology: Synchronicity and the Self*. New York: Harper and Row, 1979.

Bradshaw, John. *Healing the Shame That Binds You*. Deerfield Beach: Health Communications, 1988.

Branden, Nathaniel. *The Disowned Self*. New York: Bantam, 1988.

————. *The Psychology of Self-Esteem*. New York: Bantam, 1987.

Buber, Martin. *I and Thou*. New York: Scribner Classic, 1987.

Campbell, Joseph. *Hero with a Thousand Faces*. Princeton: Princeton University Press, 1968.

————. *Myths To Live By*. New York: Bantam, 1988.

————. *The Power of Myth*. New York: Doubleday, 1988.

Capra, Fritjof. *The Tao of Physics*. New York: Bantam, 1988.

Davis, Madelaine and Wallbridge, David. *Boundary and Space: An Introduction to the Work of D.W. Winnicott*. New York: Brunner-Mazel. 1981.

Edinger, Edward, *Anatomy of the Psyche*. La Salle: Open Court Press, 1985.

————. *Ego and Archetype*. New York: Penguin, 1986.

Eliade, Mircea. *Shamanism: Archaic Techniques of Ecstasy*. Princeton: Bollinger, 1964.

Eliot, Alexander, et al. *Universal Myths*. New York: New American Library, 1976.

Frankl, Viktor. *The Unheard Cry for Meaning*. New York: Washington Square Press, 1978.

Fromm, Erich. *The Art of Loving*. New York: Harper, 1956.

Gendlin, Eugene. *Focusing*. New York: Bantam, 1980.

Herrigel, Eugen. *Zen and the Art of Archery*. New York: Random House, 1981.

Hillman, James. *The Dream and the Underworld*. New York: Harper and Row, 1979.

Johnson, Robert. *Inner Work: Using Dreams and Active Imagination for Personal Growth*. New York: Harper and Row, 1986.

Jung, Carl. *Memories, Dreams, and Reflections*. New York: Random-Vantage, 1989.

————. *Psychology and Alchemy*. Princeton: Princeton University Press, 1968.

————, et al. *Man and His Symbols*. New York: Bantam, 1964.

Masterson, James. *The Search for the Real Self*. New York: Free Press, 1989.

Mattoon, Mary Ann. *Understanding Dreams*. Dallas: Spring, 1984.

Miller, Alice. *Drama of the Gifted Child*. New York: Basic Books, 1981.

———. *Thou Shalt Not Be Aware*. New York: Farrar, Straus and Giroux, 1984.

Polster, Erving and Miriam. *Gestalt Therapy Integrated*. New York: Random House, 1974.

Sanford, John. *Invisible Partners*. Mahwah: Paulist Press, 1980.

Scarf, Maggie. *Intimate Partners*. New York: Ballantine Books, 1988.

Smith, Manuel J. *When I Say No I Feel Guilty*. New York: Bantam, 1989.

Suzuki, Shunryu. *Zen Mind, Beginner's Mind*. New York: Weather-hill, 1976.

Trungpa, Chogyam. *Cutting Through Spiritual Materialism*. Berkeley: Shambhala, 1973.

Von Franz, Marie-Louise. *On Dreams and Death*. Boston: Shambhala, 1984.

Wilber, Ken. *No Boundary*. Boston: Shambhala, 1981.

———. *Spectrum of Consciousness*. Wheaton: Theosophical Publications, 1977.

———, et al. *Transformations of Consciousness*. Boston: Shambhala, 1986.

Audio Cassettes by David Richo, Ph.D.

Dr. Richo gives classes and retreats which are often taped. They explore the subjects in this book in greater detail. If you would like a catalog, please send a self-addressed, stamped, legal-sized envelope to:

CASSETTES
Box 31027
Santa Barbara, CA 93130

Visit website for catalog at davericho.com

Also by David Richo

WHEN LOVE MEETS FEAR
How to Become Defense-less
and Resource-full

The author of How to Be an Adult examines the deepest roots of fear and explains how they cripple our ability to release our full potential. He presents a concrete program of change for handling fear both physically and spiritually. Integrating Freudian and Jungian psychology with Christian and Buddhist spirituality, Richo shows readers how to become defense-less, allowing themselves to feel fear without buffering defenses, and how to be resource-full, learning to act in new ways. In the end, working through fears reveals the path to loving and being loved.

Paper $14.95   0-8091-3702-X

available from your bookstore or from
Paulist Press
997 Macarthur Boulevard
Mahwah, NJ 07430

www.paulistpress.com

Visit website for catalog at da
vericho.com